To Andrew
All the Best

Dedicated to my wife Pam, my daughter

Lauren, my son Gregor, my granddaughter

Lilly and my best friend

Alan Ross

What the f*** were you playing at?
Written by James Oliver

This is a biographical work.
The events and conversations in this book have been set down
to the best of the author's ability to recall them.

ISBN 978-0-9928825-6-3

Niall Harkiss

First Edition: May 2021
Second Edition: August 2021

Book layout and design by K & N Concepts Ltd
www.facebook.com/kandnconcepts

What the f*** were you playing at?

James Oliver

Acknowledgements

I would like to thank the following people who committed to purchasing the book. Without your support it would have been difficult to gauge what interest there may have been for it.

Dale Finlayson, Brian Duncan, Neil Jackson, Alex Dunbar, Donald Munro, Neil Young, Jim Goodman, David Nimmons, Martin MacBean, William Macrae, Michael Morris, Morag Sutherland, Colin Thomson, Kevin-Kyle Paton-Oakes, Alice & Bruce Gordon, Stuart Reid, Ian McNeill, Steve McHattie, Fiona Sutherland, Jillian Walker, George Campbell, Donald Wilson, Emma Maclennan, John Murray, Calum Macleod, Colin Macleod, Luke Bunch, Graham Gordon, Rosanne Mackay, Murdo Morrison, Derek MacRae, Eileen & Denis Bridgeford, Ray Goller, Martin Fraser, Karen Hercher, Callum Mackay, Rhona & Kevin Clyne, Lynn Buchan, John Skinner, David Taylor, James Manson, Joanna Mackinnon, Donald Cameron, Agnes Maclennan, Michael MacRae, Mark Mitchell, Willie Mckenzie, Darren Woolam, Yvonne Urquhart, Derek Mackenzie, William Corbett, Barrie Buchan, Allan Ross, Finlay Noble, Brian Neish, Frank Strang, Angela Spence, Gordon Robertson, Chris Cooper, Samantha Ross, Roy Cattanach, Malcom Macleod, Darren Pullen, Ian Hair, Steve Cook, Stevie Paterson, Carol Ross, Will Ross, Les Wilson, Joan Murray, Colin Lind, Eric & Anne-Marie Stuart, Neil Connell, John Cameron, Kevin Cheesman, Stuart Nichol, Billy Read, Graham Sutherland, David Mackay, Kevin Sephton, Karl Mair, Robert Ross, Donald

Hugh Mackay, Jay Bastian, Tara MacDonald, Lana & Neil Shepherd, Gavin Dearie, Erin Murphy, Stephan Pater, Duncan Black, Liam Kidney, Jean & Bill Bauman, Paul Manson, James Conway, Mary Murray, Dave McGinlay, Laurie Mackay, Michael Innes, Dusty Vass, Ian Campbell, Kenneth Macgregor, Dean Higgins, Graeme Giles, Chris Barry, Jeanette & Edwin Skinner, Stuart Davidson, Diane Matheson, Murdo Macleod, Stewart Patience, William Burgess, George Beedie, Martyn Ross, Donald Sutherland, Jacqueline MacDonald, Mo Black, Norma & Ian Sommerville, Bob Shepherd, Maureen & Will Ross, Debbie Oliver & Dave Magee, George & Elizabeth Oliver, Alan Boath, Tricia Sharp, Willie Oliver, Alison Skitt, Ian "Macspooch" MacDonald, John Cowling, John MacDonald, John Stewart, Brian Oliver, John Grant, Gary Scott, Iain Gray, Gordon Simpson, Alison Gordon, Andrew Scobbie, Emma Macfarlane, Elaine Ross & June Ripley, Carole & David Ross, Laurence Macrae, Suzanne Hastings, Rosie & Brian Urquhart, E J Kennedy, Lesley Conner, Catherine Gallagher, Hazel & Alan Bell, Maureen MacKay, Neil Hampton, Rachel & Chris Lynam, Shari & Donald Ross, Dennis MacKay, Ian Mackay, Archie Coffield, Andrew Patience, Allan Mackay, Kate Simpson, Sian & Sandy Mackenzie, Anthony Ward, Graham Rae, Danny Macrae, Di Wood, Andrew Davidson, Laura & John Dundas, Olivia & Dave Fraser, Eileen & Eric Morrison, Andrew MacDonald, Alex McFarlane, Dave Penman, Dave Penman Jnr, Marc Penman, Steve Shaddick, Jim Kirkwood, John Wood & Bobby Livingstone

Thank you to every one of you and of course to Niall Harkiss of K N Concepts as you helped me to achieve something that I had thought about for a long time.

JO

Introduction

In June 2020, after nearly 3 months in Lockdown due to the Covid-19 Pandemic, I was at a stage where the main tasks were done. The garden was in good shape, all the little jobs around the house that Pam had been niggling away at me to do for years had been done and now I had time on my hands. I am a compulsive collector and if I am at an event, I will take something to remind me of the event. I would take it home and throw it in to a box. When that box was full, I would put it up in the loft and start another box. Now it was time to sort out the boxes that I had saved up over the years.

As I sifted through around 10 boxes that had a collection of photos, programmes, event tickets, letters, football contracts, employment information I thought that I should get them in to some sort of order. The three main categories I separated them under were Personal, Work and Events. Under the events I put Football and soon this pile started growing more than the others as all my football memorabilia piled up.

I thought that I would categorize the football memorabilia by team and this got me to create a list of the teams that I had played for throughout my playing career. I have had several more years involvement with football after I finished playing but for me anything other than playing was just a poor substitute for actually being on the park.

As I created the list, I got to around 15 teams that I had played for and was remembering some of the characters whom I had played with, played against and the Managers I had played for. Although there were some periods where the football was not great and my ability or discipline was in question, I mostly remember having a great time.

So I decided to sit and record my football playing journey. Football was a huge part of my life and if only my family read this at least they will see what it meant to me and how it made me the person I am. Maybe that is good thing maybe it is a bad thing!

What I do think of my time in football is that it allowed me to meet many lifelong friends, allowed me to rub shoulders with some of football's giants, helped me in my business life and built in me a strong team ethos. There are many people whom I have met on this journey that helped me and I may not have mentioned them in the book. To all those who have helped me I thank you and I hope that you enjoy reading about my football journey. From the young boy who asked his friends if he could join in their game to the 55-year-old who signed off with a goal in his last 11 a side game I hope you enjoy some of the stories.

By the way the title of my book "What the f*** were you playing at?" comes from a quote from one of my managers who was giving me a dressing down at the time. It is what I think of when I think of him and it could possibly be used to describe several of the situations I got in to on my journey.

JO

Chapter 1

The Kick Off

My first football memory was in Primary 4 at school and that was to be the start of a lifetime of falling in and out of love with the game.

I asked if I could join in a game of football the other boys were playing in and they said I could get a game if I went in goals. This was the position that you were given if you were hopeless or carrying too much weight…

At that age I was not carrying too much weight, so it must have been that I was hopeless! I joined in and enjoyed it and I was then a regular in the playground games. As I got to know the game, I gradually got a little bit better. The fact that I could only get a game in goals to begin with spurred me on to get better.

I was brought up in the Easter Ross area of the Highlands of Scotland in a small village called Hilton. Hilton was one of the three Seaboard Villages and the other two were Balintore and Shandwick. Shandwick has a beautiful mile long sandy beach and the area is sometimes called the Ross-shire Riviera. It was a fantastic place to grow up in and as kids we were always out playing in the fresh air and in the summer, we were never out of the water. We would go out in the morning and not come home until teatime and during the day we would be in and out of our friends' houses getting snacks to keep us going. The villages have a proud footballing history with teams such as the Seaside Swifts, Seaside Rovers, Seaboard United and Balintore winning many local leagues and cups over the years and producing many players that went on to play at higher levels. My first influence in football was Auntie Meg or Maggie Jane Ross to give her full name. We called her Auntie Meg although she was not really our Auntie. She used to baby sit my older sister, myself and my younger brother on Saturday nights when my parents would go out. My father played in a band and they played throughout the Highlands and sometimes my mother would go with him if they were playing locally. Auntie Meg's payment for looking after us was a half-bottle of whisky and 20 No.6 fags. She was Rangers daft and I got to stay up and watch the football on Saturday nights when she would be shouting at the TV if her beloved Rangers were on TV. Therefore, as a youngster there was only one team I could support, and I grew up a Rangers supporter while in school. I was to break Meg's heart by changing my allegiance to another team in my late teens.

When I was in Primary 6 someone who was to become a huge influence in my football career came to be a teacher at our school. John Jackson had played professional football at Dundee United and he had moved North to take up a teaching placement at our school. He moved in to a house in Balintore and he was an English teacher in Hilton Junior Secondary School. Back in those days the teachers would give up their own time after school to help develop the school football team and John put in a power of work with all the teams at the school. The amount of time that he invested in the Hilton School players during school time and after school with the older village players was to leave a lasting legacy in the villages. John tragically died in a car crash outside Tain in 1976.

We played football all the time and would play during breaks at school and then on the football pitch in Balintore. The pitch in Balintore used to be on the outskirts of the village beside Rovers Crescent and was always being used. The youngsters would go there straight from school and then the older lads would arrive home from work with their piece bags. There would sometimes be about 15 a-side and we would play until it was dark. It was great playing against the older lads as you had to learn quickly to look after yourself.

The football pitch was surrounded on two sides by Balintore Farm fields and sometimes there were sheep or cows in the fields. The fences were not very good at keeping them out and they liked to get in to eat the lush grass. This resulted in there being quite a bit of sheep and cows shit dropped on the pitch. Before the game could go ahead, we would have to get the shit off the park but there were always some bits you could not get. The local name for the shit was sharn and should the ball go in to some the shout went up "Sharn on the Ball". This was the signal for everyone to stop where they were and the person who was in possession had to clean the sharn off the ball on the grass. You were not allowed to move when this was being done but inevitably people would be trying to gain some advantage by moving in to a better position. It was deemed unsporting to shout "Sharn on the Ball" as someone was about to head for goals but it was done and seeing someone trying to pull out from heading the potentially shit covered ball was hilarious.

I was brought up first of all in Shore Street in Hilton and when I was about 9 the family moved out in to the countryside at Cadboll. We had a big garden and my brother George and I pestered our father to make some football goals for us so that we could practice. My cousin Derek Wood lived next door and he joined in as well and sometimes at weekends we had our pals up and played for hours. Derek was 3 years older than me and it helped me to grow physically playing against him as he was a big strong lad and at that age it was a huge difference. The goals my father got made for us were basically 5 a side goals about 4 foot high and 6 yards wide but they were like the best football goals in the world to us.

All this extra football helped me to progress and by the time I was in Primary 7 I was team Captain. This was a great transformation in a little over 2 years from the guy who was deemed only good enough to play in goals. I now played Central Midfield and we won the Ross-shire Primary School League. I was what you would call a box-to-box player (something which would surprise a few of my colleagues in later teams I played in!). I remember we were presented with the Heathmount Cup by the local Conservative MP Alastair MacKenzie. My team mates in that first Championship winning team were James (Alec) Ross, Alfred Mackay, Robert Allan, John Vass, Harry McBride, Andrew MacDonald, Jim Robb, George Oliver (Brother), James Vass, George Wood and Alexander MacAngus.

While still in the Primary part of Hilton Junior Secondary School I played for the school Under 15's team. John Jackson was in charge of our school teams and he was not frightened to put me in against guys that were about 3 or 4 years older than me. At that age there was a huge physical difference but I know that it toughened me up and I also know that some of the older lads looked out for me.

In 1970 I moved to Tain Royal Academy when I went in to 1st year. Tain was a Senior Secondary school while Hilton was one of the last Junior Secondary Schools. 2 years later the Junior Secondary section of Hilton School closed and it became just a Primary School with all senior pupils moving directly to Tain School. As John Jackson taught in the Junior Secondary part, he was transferred to Tain where he got involved in the football again.

When I went to Tain at first I played for their Under 13's and Under 14's while in 1st year but was overlooked for their Under 15's as there were lots of older more physical players to choose from. This was when John Jackson (while he was still at Hilton) approached Tain school asking if I could play for Hilton Under 15's as they were needing some players. This was to be my first and only experience of being a "loan player". I was on loan from Tain to Hilton and actually played against Tain for them.

I also remember at this time playing against Roddie MacDonald, who went on to play for Celtic and Hearts, as he played for Invergordon Academy. He was immense and far too strong for someone like me who was a few years younger. He was even too strong for most of our guys who were the same age as him. This convinced me that I needed to be stronger. My father had a building business and I would be using concrete blocks as weights to build myself up. I was stronger than most of the guys my age and this helped me to look after myself on the park. I was now starting to play against adults and had to grow up very quickly.

Around this time, I was training with Seaboard United a team from the Seaboard Villages under the guidance of John Jackson. The villages had been without a football team for several years until John whipped up support from a number of locals to get a team in to the Ross-shire Welfare League.

The biggest game of the year for the village team was the Carnival Cup Final. It was called the final even though it was a one-off game. It was played on the Saturday evening of the Seaboard Gala Week when the village team played the team from the local town of Tain. Several of the Village team plied their skills for the likes of Invergordon, Alness and Tain in the North Reserve league (now North Caledonian League) but they all came and played this game for the village team.

I remember being so excited to be told that I and my friend Graham (Coochie) Skinner would be playing in our first Carnival Cup Final at the tender ages of 14 and 15 respectively. We won 3-2 and I scored 2 and Graham got the other. What a buzz that was.

Graham was a fantastic player and I have no doubt that he would have

Hilton Primary School – Ross-shire League Winners 1969/70
Back Row L to R: Andrew MacDonald, James Robb, Robert Allan, George Oliver,
James Vass & George Wood
Front Row L to R: John Vass, Alexander MacAngus, James Oliver, James Ross, Alfred
MacKay & Harry McBride

become a very good professional player if he had got the opportunity. More about this later.

When I moved into 2nd Year I was involved in the Tain Under 14 and Under 15 squads so my "Loan" to Hilton came to an end. The nucleus of our Under 15 team made up the bulk of the Inver Under 16's team. This was run by Edwin Skinner and Don MacMillan. Edwin is still involved in kid's football in Ross-shire 52 years later! He has spent a lifetime supporting football in the Easter Ross area and should be given some official recognition of his input. Don was an ex Celtic and Aberdeen player who had been playing for Ross County and he was renowned for the power of his shooting.

I did not play too many games for the Inver team in my first year as there was again a bit of an age gap and physically wise there were bigger stronger players to pick from. I was however to play a key role in the team winning the league that year.

We needed 3 points from our last 2 games to win the league from Conon. I was substitute for our game away to Avoch and at half time we were 3-0 down. Don wanted to put me in goals (I still enjoyed a game in goals now and again at training) as our regular keeper was not playing well.

Edwin said "We need goals, put him on at Centre Forward".

He won the debate and I scored a second half hat trick to get us a 3-3 draw to take it to the last game of the season.

The game was away to our nearest rivals Conon Bridge. Despite my goal scoring heroics of the previous week, I was again on the bench and with the score 4-3 to us I was put on in goals!

In the last minute we gave away a penalty. The Conon player looked nervous as he had the kick to possibly win the league but I dived the right way and held the ball and a few minutes later it was all over and we were Ross-shire Under 16 champions. That was my last game in goals although

I used to enjoy going in goals at shooting practice at later clubs. I think I would have been not too bad a keeper but I would have been bored to tears plus I don't think I was mad enough to be a goalie.

The following year I was to concentrate on being an outfield player. My preferred position was centre of midfield but I had an eye for scoring goals and I was asked to play upfront for Inver Under 16's. I was still playing Centre of Midfield for the school and getting a few goals from there as well. I had been on a school cruise to the Baltic the year before and had met some great friends from Lewis there. Each year there was a game of football between the Ross-shire Under 15's Select and the Lewis Under 15's Select. I was desperate to win a place in the select team as the game this year was in Stornoway. I was successful in the selection matches for the team and I was looking forward to going over to Lewis to play against the Lewis Select. Two days before I was due to go on the trip, I was going over a ramp on my bike and I came off it and came down in an almighty heap. I could hardly move my arm but kept quiet about it and turned up at the meeting point at Dingwall. We were staying in Dingwall that night as we were due to get an early bus to Ullapool and then a boat across the Minch to Stornoway. The Dingwall PE teacher who was in charge of us asked me if I was alright as he thought I was in a bit of pain. I said I was OK and that it was just a bit stiff after straining it in school. We got the bus to Ullapool and the ferry to Stornoway and the friends I met on the cruise were there to meet the boat when it came in to Stornoway. They were convinced that the Lewis Select would beat us as they said there were some great players in their team.

The game was played at Goathill Park and I played for the first half but had to come off at half time as I was in agony. We won the game 5-2 but I felt bad because I could not play properly. I went out at night with my friends and some of the other Ross-shire lads and we ended up at the YMCA disco. These guys were Islanders and they had got their hands on some booze and

I think that was my first drink after a game. With the drink inside me I forgot about the pain in my shoulder and when I woke up the next day, I was in agony but could not work out what was the sorest my head or my shoulder.

When I got back home, I went to my doctor and was sent for an x-ray and it was revealed that I had broken my collar bone in the bike crash. This kept me out of the North of Scotland Schoolboy selection matches and by not getting in to that you did not get in to the Scottish Schoolboy selection process. I don't know if I would have got there but it would have been great to have had the opportunity.

It really was a great time to be growing up and we were always out in the fresh air running, cycling or swimming but most of all kicking and chasing a football. I would not change the childhood I had for what the kids have nowadays in a million years.

Inver Under 16's receive their Ross-shire Under 16's Championship trophy and medals from Ally MacLeod who was Manager of Ayr United at that time

Back Row L to R: Stephen, Alan Marshall, Gordon Mackay, William Ross, Jack MacKay, Ian MacDonald, Gordon Smith, Leslie Stein, James Oliver & David Ross

Front Row L to R: Jamie McJimpsey, Russell Marshall, Ally MacLeod, Bruce Paterson & Donald Hugh MacKay

The Ross-shire Under 16 Champions Medal 1970-71

Chapter 2

Up to 17 Year Old

Don MacMillan, one of the Inver Under 16 coaches, was given the Manager's job at Brora Rangers and he took 3 of his Inver Under 16's with him. We were classed as S-signings. This was the old Schoolboy forms which tied us to the club. The other 2 players were a year older than me, Jack Mackay from Inver and Dave Ross from Tain.

Dave was an excellent player and went on to become a great full back with Brora and Ross County before work took him away to England. We trained at Brora 2 nights a week with the team's Highland League players. Back then there was no Dornoch Bridge and we had to go round by Ardgay and Bonar Bridge before being dropped off at Tain around 11.30pm. My mother or father would pick me up and take me the seven miles to the villages.

We did this for a while but at this time Brora did not have a regular reserve side and games were few and far between. As I was signed on as an S-signing I was not allowed to play for anyone else and I was getting frustrated at not playing on a Saturday. I remember it came to a head one Saturday as I was asked to join the first team squad and was told I would be involved in a game at Lossiemouth and with 2 mins to go and down 4-0 I was asked to get stripped and I was not too happy. I did not go on - so that does not count as my Highland League debut!

On Saturdays I used to go and watch Tain St Duthus playing as some of my school pals Alan Ross, James Weir and Gordon Murray were playing there. It was frustrating to be sitting watching games that I knew I could be playing in. John Jackson was the coach of the St Duthus team at the time and one of the Senior Players was Bob Bannerman.

At the same time Mr Smythe, the rector at Tain Royal Academy was getting reports from a teacher about me being very tired at school. Mr Smythe wrote to Brora Rangers to request that my S-signing be cancelled as the late nights were taking its toll on my schooling. I often wonder who the teacher was that asked the Rector to request my release? Could it have been a certain Mr Jackson? Brora duly agreed and I signed for Tain who had John Jackson training them for the start of season 1974-75.

That summer I played for Inver Under 16's again, but this time as an out and out centre forward. We played in the North Section against Invergordon, Firth United, Alness and Black Rock Rovers. Ourselves and Invergordon were the two top teams in our group. Playing for Invergordon was a player who was to go on to become very well known throughout Scottish football and someone I was to bump into many times in the next almost 40 years. Yes, top football commentator Rob MacLean was a striker for Invergordon then.

We had been scoring freely against the other teams and had won 2-1 in Invergordon and we were playing them on a Friday night at Inver in what would be the section decider. With our last game at home to Firth United, whom we had already beaten 14-0, a draw or win against Invergordon would surely be enough to get us the top spot.

At this time, I had started training with Ross County on a Sunday morning. There were some of the Invergordon boys training as well. I was first to be picked up at around 8.00am and we would pick up others in Kildary,

Invergordon and Alness on the way through to Dingwall.

Ian McNeill the Ross County Manager asked us how we thought the game would go on the Friday night. The Invergordon boys said that they thought that we had robbed them in Invergordon and that they were going to get revenge. This spurred me on and it helped us to a very convincing win to top the North Section.

When we turned up for training on the Sunday after the Friday night game Mr McNeill asked us what the score was in the game. I had great delight in telling him that we had won 11-1.

"Did you manage to get a goal or two?" he asked me.

"Just the eight!" was my answer, in front of the cringing Invergordon guys. I think he already knew the outcome but was giving me a chance to rub it in.

In our last game we beat Firth United 23-0 and I managed to get 11 goals in that game. I almost got a quadruple hat trick after lobbying their keeper in the last minute but my mate Gordon Murray smashed it over the line for his first goal of the season in fact possibly his first ever goal. I don't think I will ever forgive him for that.

I finished the 8-game section with 40 goals in the 8 games an incredible average of 5 goals per game and this was something that I was and still am very proud of. As we won the North Section, we had to play Avoch in the final as they had won the South Section. There was however to be disappointment for us in the final as Avoch beat us 2-1 in the final. They had a centre forward playing for them called Ross Jack who went on to have a great career in football. Ross played for teams such as Everton, Norwich, Dunfermline and Dundee and is now a colleague at ICTFC as he is heavily involved in the Academy set up. More about Ross soon as we gained our revenge on the Avoch lads.

I could not get enough football and was playing for our School team on

Saturday mornings, for Tain St Duthus in the afternoon and we also had school games and Inver Under 16's games through the week. Tain Royal Academy and Fortrose Academy were the two top School teams at that time and it came down to us needing to win at Fortrose to win the Ross-shire Schools league.

The bulk of the Inver Under 16's team went to Tain while all of the Avoch team were at Fortrose. The Fortrose PE teacher Jack Sutherland was a strict disciplinarian and he hated anyone beating his teams. He was referee for this game and we knew that we would not get any favours.

I scored 2 goals as we went 3-0 up at half time. Just after halftime I ran on to a pass from my own half and was clear with only the keeper to beat when he blew the whistle. I asked what he had blown for and he told me that I was offside. I told him that I could not have been offside as I was in my own half when the ball was played. He started shouting at me and I called him a "F**king Cheat" and booted the ball as far away as I could. He told me to go and get it and I told him to go and get it himself. He sent me off and I had to walk back to the changing rooms at Fortrose school.

As I was walking back our PE Teacher Jim MacGregor was walking towards me and he asked me if I was injured. I had to tell him that I had been sent off. He asked me what I had been sent off for and I told him that I called the referee a cheat for blowing for offside when I wasn't. He immediately gave me a clip round the ear for being sent off. When he spoke to the Fortrose PE Teacher and found out the whole extent of what had happened, he was raging and told me to report to him the next day.

We had held on to win 3-2 and we had gained some revenge for our Under16 defeat by Avoch. The next day I reported to Mr MacGregor's office and he was still mad with me and I was given 6 of the belt. He also told me that he was considering banning me from playing for the school again. As I was walking out of his room he said "well done on the goals, I heard they were crackers".

The North Reserve League had started up and I was playing for Tain St Duthus. It was great to be getting regular football. The team were in the bottom half of the league but we had some very good players. I played up front with Tommy Morrison and Ian (Banan) MacDonald and the two of them made lots of chances for me. I ended that season with around 30 goals. Adding my 40 Under 16 goals and a few more for the school that gave me 70+ in around a year and this got the attention of clubs down south.

Around this time my love affair with lager started and the Tain lads used to take me to the pub with them after the games. We would have a few beers before hitting whatever local dances were on. No names can be divulged but one player would take us in his car, before he got too drunk, to wherever the dance was. Then when we were ready to go home, he would phone the Police station and get his pals to come out and one policeman would drive his car home with a few of us in it and the rest would pile into the Police car. Community policing at its best.

It was a bit weird being out having a few beers on a Saturday night as a 16-year-old with one of your teachers!! However, it got even weirder one night when I ended up in the Balnagown Hotel in Tain with about 4 of my teachers after going there with Mr Jackson. It was extremely weird sitting in class on Monday knowing that you had been drinking and dancing with two of your female teachers on the Saturday night!

Tain had a free week one week and Ian McNeill the Ross County Manager asked me if I fancied playing a trial match for them. It was a big step up to play in the Highland League but I was delighted to take on the challenge. John and Bob at Tain were ok for me to play but told me not to sign anything.

On the day Ross County were playing Deveronvale in Dingwall. I remember lining up up front with Ross Jack in what was a very young forward line. Not long after the game started a cross came in and I was right behind Ross ready to nod the ball in to the net but he got there in front of me.

I had to wait until the 90th minute to get my goal. It was 3-3 at the time and after a great through ball myself and the goalkeeper clashed on the edge of the 18 yard box. As I went flying over him, I looked round and the ball was running towards me. I just had to lift my leg and let it run past me then knock it in to the empty net to make it 4-3 to County. I was convinced that I had scored the winner in my Highland League debut but Vale went up the other end and got an injury time equaliser.

I had never ever given becoming a professional footballer any thoughts as I was just enjoying playing football and the craic that came with it. Bob Bannerman and John Jackson took me aside at training one night and said that some clubs had been contacting them about me.

"What for?" I said.

"They want you to go on trial with them."

I actually had to ask what that meant! They told me that Tottenham Hotspur were very keen to take me to London to see what I can do. Recalling now what my reaction was, it was like I was in shock and couldn't really take in what was being said. At the same time Ian McNeill was back in touch and asked me if I wanted to play for them in some pre-season friendly games for Ross County against Celtic and Motherwell, which I did.

In the game against Celtic, I had the honour and pleasure of playing on the same pitch as Kenny Dalglish and I can still remember a chest pass that he delivered to an overlapping Danny McGrain. The pass was perfectly timed so that McGrain never broke his stride. That was a great lesson to me on how you can use your body to link play.

In the game against Motherwell, I learnt another lesson but this one was much more painful. I was outside the box waiting to make my run in to the penalty box at a corner and the ball was flighted perfectly and I was imagining the ball nestling in the back of the net. However, I then woke up in the dressing room. The big centre half for Motherwell Willie McVie had checked my run in to the box and I met up with his elbow and it was Goodnight Vienna. Very sore but it taught me to have my arms in a position to fend off defenders. All good experience. I was to have the opportunity for revenge against McVie in the not-too-distant future.

Bob Bannerman and John Jackson said it would be good experience for me but whatever I did don't sign anything. They were like my agents!

I remember the day the invite arrived from Tottenham and I still have the letter in my scrap book. I got off the school bus and my mother came out the door of the house waving a white letter. I think she was more excited than I was. My older sister Maureen and my brother George were there as they also came off the school bus. I did not want to open it until my father was there so we waited until he came home. The letter was from the assistant Manager Wilf Dixon and they were inviting me down to London after getting reports from their scout in Scotland. I had to write back to them and tell them when I was available and a date was set for me to go down.

Bob Bannerman told me that Dundee United had also been in touch and would like me to come down for a week-long trial with them. Bob said this would be good as it would give me some experience of being on trial at a professional football club before going to London. In the next couple of weeks, I was made aware that Leicester City and Ipswich Town had both been in touch wanting me to go on trial with them also. There were also reports in the local paper that Aberdeen FC were keeping an eye on me.

It was shaping up to be a busy time for me. I was still thinking that I would soon be going back to school to sit my Highers as my plan was to become a Civil Engineer. My father was in the Building Industry as was his

TELEPHONE: 01-808 2046   TELEGRAMS: TOTHOTSPUR·LONDON N17

TOTTENHAM HOTSPUR FOOTBALL & ATHLETIC CO. LTD.

MEMBERS OF THE FOOTBALL ASSOCIATION AND THE FOOTBALL LEAGUE

LEAGUE CHAMPIONS
1951   1961
LEAGUE CUP WINNERS
1971   1973
SECRETARY: G.W.JONES

748 HIGH ROAD
TOTTENHAM·N17 OAP
CHAIRMAN: SIDNEY A.WALE

WINNERS OF F.A. CUP
1901, 1921, 1961, 1962
1967
MANAGER: ~~W.E.NICHOLSON~~
W.J.T.NEILL

WD/JMH   27th May 1975.

J. Oliver, Esq.,
Torridon,
Fearn,
Nr. Tain,
Rosshire,
Scotland.

Dear Jimmy,

    On the recommendation of Mr. R. Bannerman and my scout, Mr. Florence in Scotland, we would like to extend an invitation for you to come to England, if at all possible, for a week during our pre-season training period some time in July.

    I hope that this proposal coincides with your holidays, but if so, would you please write to me and give me some idea of the best time for you to come, and no doubt we can come to some arrangement.

    Wishing you well for the summer, and I look forward to hearing from you.

                Yours truly,

                Wilf Dixon
                <u>Asst. Manager.</u>

Busy time for James

IT IS going to be a happy new soccer season for 18-year-old James Oliver from the Ross-shire village of Fearn. For James will lead the Ross County attack against Motherwell on Saturday and Blackpool on Monday . . . and will then fly to London for a week's trial with Tottenham Hotspur, writes **Bill McAllister.**

James is earmarked by County to fill the scoring boots of John Wilkie, transferred to Elgin City for £3500 —but Spurs manager Terry Neill has been tipped off about the lad and wants to look.

Oliver caught the eye playing for Tain in the North Reserve League, and Ross County moved for him at the end of last season.

Ross manager Ian McNeill said last night: "James is a fine prospect and I've decided to give him his chance as a striker, starting against Motherwell at Victoria Park this Saturday.

"He will take John Wilkie's place and will form a front trio with experienced Ian Hunter and Jim Fleming. James can also play midfield and is a lad I think we'll hear a lot more about."

TIP-OFF

Oliver will miss County's match with Partick Thistle next Wednesday because that day he flies to London to report to White Hart Lane.

The Spurs invitation has come following a tip-off to Tottenham from Tain player-coach Bob Bannerman, the former Ross County and Brora inside man.

Inswich Town are also interested and want the lad to visit them when he can manage.

It certainly looks like being a hectic start for the Easter Ross youngster!

County are delighted with the form of ex-Dunfermline wing half Charlie Brine, signed on two months' trial, in private, practice matches and Brine will play against Motherwell.

The Fir Park side, who play Clach next Monday and Brora on Tuesday, will use their North tour to blood their £80,000 worth of new recruits — centre half Willie McVie from Clyde and strikers Colin MacAdam from Dumbarton and Vic Davidson from Celtic.

father before him. My mother's father Alex Ross was also a builder, so our family were steeped in the Construction sector. I used to love going up to the West Coast as a youngster to visit my grandparents in Poolewe as we had to pass some of the massive Hydro Electric dams that were built there in the 50's & 60's. I always wanted to be involved in building something like that and my favourite subjects at school were Engineering Drawing, Engineering Science and of course Physical Education.

With a couple of weeks to go before I was to go away on trials Bob arranged for me to play for his old village team Gairloch to keep me fit. Gairloch were playing in the Wester Ross Amateur league and were in a cup semi-final against one of their local rivals.

Myself and my friend Alan Ross went up on the Saturday morning as it was a Saturday evening kick off. We were to stay in Bob's fathers house in Gairloch but the game was to be played in nearby Aultbea.

The pitch was not the biggest in the world and I recall there was a player in the Gairloch team called John Kirby who had a very long throw in. Nearly every throw in we got in their half was like having a corner and we won 8-2 and I managed to score 4 of them to take the team through to the Cup Final the following week.

After the game the team went back to the Drumachork Hotel for refreshments. This hotel had the longest bar I had ever seen and the interesting thing about it was that there were only 2 beer taps at one end. There was a fantastic array of whiskies behind the bar and this seemed to be the only thing the locals were drinking.

There was a group of older men sitting at a table and they shouted me over. They said that they had heard my surname was Oliver and they asked if I was any relation to Jimmy Oliver who used to live in Poolewe. My Grandmother Margaret had been the school teacher there and I told them that he was my grandfather. They told me that they were his pals and could

Gairloch 1975

Back Row L to R: Roddy MacLeod, Cathel MacAskill, Ken Alick MacLennan, Charlie Robb, Roy MacKenzie, Duncan MacKenzie & Raymond Gault
Front Row L to R: Murray Ross, Roddy MacKenzie, James Oliver, John Kirby, Willie MacRae & Tommy O'Hara

they get me a drink. I don't remember much more about that night.

The following week we came up for the Cup Final which was being played at the same venue. We played a strong team from the Contin area and got beaten by the odd goal. This week there were two more friends my cousin Murray Ross and Gordon Murray with us as we had decided that we would camp out in Gairloch and enjoy the summer weather and the tourist season. We did however make the fundamental mistake of not putting the tent up before we went to the pub. We made some sort of attempt to put it up when we eventually got back to the camp site. It was not a very successful attempt as I remember waking up with cloth over my face and thinking holy shit am I in the morgue. The tent had collapsed through the night and was draped over the top of the four of us. As we got up from under the tent, we could tell by their looks that the other campers had been having a good laugh at our expense.

It was arranged that I go on trial at Tannadice the week before I went to Spurs. Again, Bob said to me not to sign anything as I was going to Spurs the following week and I was just at United to sample what a football club was like. It was arranged that I would travel down to a village called Muirhead just outside Dundee on the Sunday and that I would stay with a friend of Bob's called Angus Balharry who was connected to United and he would take me in to training on the Monday morning. I think he had a brother who was a well-known naturalist called Dick Balharry. My parents left me and I spent the evening in Muirhead with the Balharry's.

The next morning, we made the short trip into Dundee and I remember thinking how big a stadium Tannadice was and that there was another stadium on the other side of the road! Angus took me in and I remember we climbed up a set of stairs and we were taken to the Manager's office.

This was the first time I met or spoke to Jim McLean the United Manager. When I think back now, I had no idea who the manager was or who any of their players were and I was about to train with them. I was taken in to the dressing room and I was introduced to some of the other younger players in the away dressing room and we were given some training gear to wear.

One of the lads who spoke to me first was a lad called Graeme Payne and we hit it off straight away and we are still friends to this day. He helped me to settle in and the banter in the room was very much like the banter in any football dressing room with someone always trying to take the mickey out of someone.

Soon we were heading off to training and all the players jumped in to various cars and soon we were up at the training parks beside the Cash Register company. We did a short warm up and then Mr McLean said that they would be playing a game 1st Team v 2nd Team.

I lined up as Centre Forward for the 2nd Team and after about 5 mins we got a corner. I liked going outside the box and making a run from the far side of the box toward the ball so that I could get maximum height. I think it was Graeme Payne who took the corner and he struck a perfect cross and I met it at the same time as the goalkeeper and the 2 centre backs. The result was that I got my head to it a fraction of a second before I hit Hamish McAlpine, Walter Smith and Jackie Copland and we all ended up in a heap in the net.

I was back at Tannadice a few years ago with clients at Hospitality. Hamish MacAlpine and John Holt were at our table that day and Hamish recalled my first day at the club. It was nice to hear him say that I had made such an impression.

So, 1-0 to us and what a way to start your week's trial. Playing up front with me that day was Henry Hall and he scored to make it 2-0 and then Andy Gray pulled one back but then I ran on to a great through ball from Henry rounded Hamish and rolled it in to the net to complete the scoring. The thing is I did not feel I had done anything different than I had been doing at Tain.

When we got back to Tannadice after the morning session Mr McLean asked me to come to his room. He told me that he wanted to sign me and being a naïve youngster from the Highlands I blurted out "Oh I am not allowed to" to which he said "Why not?" and I replied that I was only there to see what it is like at a professional football club as I was going to Spurs next week.

He never spoke to me for the rest of the week. After that explosive start the rest of the week was quieter but I really enjoyed it and I was put in to digs with another lad called Billy Kirkwood who was also on trial. I think Billy had been there a few times before and was destined to become a Tannadice legend.

In the house next door to us were two other lads who were destined to also become even bigger United Legends. The digs were in the Lochee area of Dundee and these lads were Paul Hegarty and Paul Sturrock. We all travelled in to training together that week and the others that I hung around with were Graeme Payne, John Holt and Dave Cooper. Dave was the Reserve keeper and had played for Glenrothes in their Scottish Junior Cup winning team and he was a great character. I really enjoyed hanging out with these guys that week and the fact that they made me feel so welcome was a huge factor when deciding what to do.

At the end of the week, I finished training and just left without speaking to anyone. My parents came and picked me up and took me home. I enjoyed my weeks training and I did not feel out of place although I was impressed with their 1st Team Centre Forward Andy Gray who was my type of player. He would put his head where others wouldn't put their feet to score a goal. Something I have done quite often as several broken noses, split eyelids and lost teeth will testify.

It was then a case of getting ready to go to London for my Spurs trial. I had read about some of their players and knew about Martin Chivers, Alfie Conn, Cyril Knowles, Steve Perryman, Willie Young and of course their Irish International goalkeeper the incredible Pat Jennings. There was to be one other absolute hero of mine there as well but he had left the club and was only there using the facilities to keep himself fit.

My trip to London began by going to Inverness on Sunday evening and getting on to the overnight train to London. It was a 12–13 hour journey and I was fortunate that I was able to stretch out and get a sleep. I arrived in London around 8.00am on the Monday morning and the instructions from Spurs was to get a taxi from the station to White Hart Lane and get a receipt from the driver and they would pay me back my money. I stood in the queue for a black cab and I remember the taxi seemingly taking ages to get to the ground. The fare came to around £7 and this was back in 1975.

I had £10 that my father gave me for the whole week. I remember I was a bit shocked at the price but thought it must be correct. In the moment I forgot to ask for a receipt and when I got to the Admin office and told them this, they asked how much I had paid and when I said £7 they said it should only be about half that. I had a horrible feeling that they thought I was not telling the truth and that unsettled me and the woman was asking me if I could remember the taxi number. At this point Wilf Dixon came along and said don't worry about it we will sort it out but for a young lad from the Highlands this was a telling moment.

I was taken straight to the training ground and I had never seen a place like this in my life. It was brilliant and there was about 5 training pitches and a big building that had the dressing rooms and a players' canteen.

The summer of 1975 was particularly hot and I recall the temperatures being in the 90's and it being very difficult to get to sleep at night with the humidity. That first day at training was very easy and we did not do much running but we got a lot of shooting practice. There were drink stations around the training pitches and I was drinking a lot of freezing cold milk to try and cool me down. One of the senior players said to me that maybe I should try a hot drink instead as it would make me sweat more and cool me down. At 95 degrees a Scotsman does not need anything to make him sweat.

We were sitting having our lunch when I was introduced to the lad who stayed in the digs that I was due to stay in. His name was Neil McNab and he was a Scotsman who had moved south from Greenock Morton. I remember him asking me if I wanted to go for beer and of course my answer was yes. We did only have the one though. There was another lad in the digs and his name was Paul McGrath but not the one who played for Man Utd and Ireland. The people who owned the digs were nice and friendly and they obviously looked after the boys well.

On Tuesday I was introduced to a lot of lads who were there on trial and some others who were presently with Spurs as young professionals and we played a number of games. We were told that there was a game on the Wednesday night against a local league team and that we would all be getting a run out. I can't remember who we played but it was a very tidy little ground and we won 3-1 and I managed to score a goal. The other 2 goals were scored by a guy called Hoddle; I wonder whatever happened to him?

On Thursday we were back at the training ground and at lunch time I looked over and seen one of my all-time Scottish heroes sitting at one of the tables. It was none other than the brilliant Alan Gilzean of Dundee and Scotland fame. I remember him sitting there and everyone treating him like a god. I watched him training later on as he was doing some heading practice. Then we were taken out for our afternoon session which was to be something that I will remember forever.

It was finishing practice and the goalkeeper we had to beat was none other than Pat Jennings. It was crossing and finishing, and I think I scored 5 or 6 volleys in a row and I can still remember Jennings saying in that deep Irish brogue, "We are going to have to watch this one Wilf…". Seeing Gilzean practice heading a ball and shooting practice against Pat Jennings on the one day made it a day I will never forget.

I spoke to Wilf Dixon that afternoon and he said they were very interested in me and not to decide anything until I had spoken to them. I however knew I did not want to go to London because of how the Taxi Driver had cheated me and the lady in the Administration department had not believed me. It just shows how easily people's actions can influence people decisions. I therefore left Hoddle to see what he could do at Spurs without me.

My trip back to the Highlands was another overnight journey and I got on the train at Euston and found a 6-seat compartment with no one in it and prepared to stretch out as soon as the train left the station. It was just about to leave when 5 women came in to the carriage and asked me if there was anyone else sitting there. "No", I replied in my Highland voice to which one of them said "Where are you from?"

I told them that I was from a place called Tain just North of Inverness. They said "That's great, we are from Wick, so we can share with you all the way."

I swear they never stopped talking all the bloody way from London to Inverness.

I arrived back home and was told that Spurs wanted me to come back, but my mind was made up that I wasn't going back. I was also told that Ipswich and Leicester wanted me to go on trial but I was due to go back to school on the Tuesday and this was the Friday night. I had made up my mind that I was going back to school after having mixed feelings about both trials I had been on. I liked the friendship that the United players had shown me but hated the things that happened to me at Spurs when I was so far from home. Looking back at it over the years I realise I should have gone back to school but c'est la vie.

I am a great believer that what is for you will not go by you.

Chapter 3

Dundee United

It was the Saturday night after my return from London and the phone rang in our house and my father answered it and spoke to the person on the other end for a while. He then said James that's for you. It is Mr McLean from Dundee United he would like to speak to you.

I took the phone and he asked me how I got on at Tottenham, probably knowing full well how I got on, and I told him I thought I did well and that they wanted me to come back but I would not be going as I thought it was too far from home for me. I also said that I was going to go back to school to get my Highers so that I could study Civil Engineering.

He said to me that Dundee is a lot closer than London and he would love for me to come and join them at United. He added that if I did, he would give me time off in the afternoons to attend Engineering classes at the Kingsway Technical College. He knew that I had bonded well with the guys at United and asked if myself and my parents would come and speak with him tomorrow. I spoke with my dad and he said if I wanted to go and speak, we could go. I said that we would come and see him. So, the next morning we left our house in Hilton to make the trek to Dundee to speak with him. I must have known I was going to stay as I packed some clothes and took my boots.

We rolled up to Tannadice on the Sunday and we went up to his office and we spoke about the college classes in the afternoon. He said that they had some good contacts in at the college and that they would be able to get me enrolled. He had asked his secretary to come in and have the contract prepared and I was just about to sign it when I remembered what Bob Bannerman had said to me about asking for a signing on fee. He looked startled when I asked for it and he said how much are you looking for. I said I have been told to ask for £200. £200 he exclaimed and then he mentioned that Dave Narey, Paul Sturrock and Graeme Payne had only got £70 each!! They all became United Legends so I can always say that I got almost as much as the 3 of them put together. He must have been desperate to sign me as he agreed to it without haggling.

The Secretary drew up a letter about the £200 Signing on Fee and I signed the document. We finished up and we all went outside the building. I said goodbye to my mother and father and they drove off.

Mr McLean took me to my digs in Lochee in his orange Audi and on the way said to me - "Do you drink at all?"

I thought what a strange thing to ask a 17-year-old boy from the Highlands as by that time you usually have about three years drinking under your belt! I told him that I enjoyed a pint of lager after the game to which he replied, "I don't drink at all". I sat there thinking maybe I shouldn't have said that and added "Well, actually a lager shandy…" hoping that this might make things better. There was still silence from him so I added "Well, mostly lemonade, hardly any lager", but by this time the damage was done. In later years I was to recall this as my first ever experience of "when you are in a hole, stop digging."

I was dropped off at my digs and I think it was a Mrs Clark who was the landlady. It was the same house that I had stayed in when I was down on trial. Billy Kirkwood was not there though as he had gone back to school

DUFC

THE DUNDEE UNITED FOOTBALL COMPANY LIMITED

Ground and Registered Office: Tannadice Park, Dundee
Registered in Scotland 13690
Manager: Mr J. McLean
Secretary: Mrs Helen Lindsay. Telephone Dundee 86289
Treasurer: George F. Fox, C.A., 7 Ward Road, Dundee. Telephone Dundee 24521-2

TANNADICE PARK
DUNDEE DD3 7JW

18th August 1975.

Dundee United Football Club agree to pay James D. Oliver
the sum of Two hundred pounds (£200.) as a singing on Fee.

Dundee United Football Club also agree to pay James D. Oliver
a further Two hundred and fifty pounds (£250.) if during
season 1975-76 he makes 15 appearance in the First Team Pool
of 13.   If in the event of 20 appearances, a further
Two hundred and fifty pounds (£250). will be paid.

In the event of the player not achieving either 15 or 20
appearances in season 1975-76 in the First Team Pool, then
the same agreement will be valid for season 1976-77.

Signature of Player _James Oliver_

Signature of Manager _J. McLean_

New striker for Tannadice

Dundee United last night added another promising striker to their playing staff (writes Tommy Gallacher).

He is 17-year-old, five foot 11½ inches tall, fifth year pupil at Tain Royal Academy, Jim Oliver.

Jim, who is coming to United immediately as a full-time player, was signed after talks with Jim McLean and his parents at the United ground.

Last month, Oliver, who also interested Leicester and Ipswich, spent a week at Tannadice on trial, where he created a big impression.

He has also been down at White Hart Lane, on trial with Spurs, but preferred to join Dundee United, where, although he will be a full-time player, he will continue with further education classes in the afternoons.

38

and I was to be in this house on my own. None of the other players were there as they lived close enough to Dundee that they would come straight to training on Monday mornings. As I sat in my digs alone, I wondered if I had done the right thing.

The next morning it was good to see some friendly faces and they were all pleased to see me and to hear that I had joined the club. As I was signed as a Professional Player, I did not have to do the cleaning duties that the others, who had been signed as apprentice professionals had to do. The guys who were supposed to do the cleaning of the baths, showers and washing of the kits and the cleaning of the boots were Paul Sturrock, John Holt, Dave Narey, and Graeme Payne. As they were the guys I was going to hang around with I helped them with the duties and big Dave Cooper helped us as well. We had some laughs and it helped to ease the loneliness. We would finish our duties then go down to the snooker hall for lunch and a game of snooker and a go on the pinball machine. Holty was obsessed with the pinball machine and was brilliant at it.

As I had missed the hard pre-season training, I was given extra sessions to get my fitness up and as I was pretty fit anyway this was not a problem. I then asked when I would be starting at the Kingsway Technical College and was told I would need to go and speak to them myself. This was a bit of a surprise as I thought the club were organising it. I went up and spoke to someone and eventually I got on to a Maths course two afternoons a week and there was a Tech Drawing course at night. I did it for a few weeks but I was missing some days because of training and it was difficult at night without transport so I ended up dropping the courses.

The beginning of the season was beckoning and my parents came down to see me with more clothes and some of my personal stuff that I needed. As they were about to leave, I ran after the car and stopped them.

I had asked my mother to take a tie down for me as we had to wear ties to the games. She had given me the tie but I had not got a clue how to tie it. I stopped the car and asked her to tie it round my neck and then I slipped it over my head without opening the knot. This was to be my tie for the next 3-4 months. The same brown tie with everything. One of the older players Andy Rolland clocked this after a few months and he undid the knot and that was me in a situation where I had to learn. There were some bad efforts before I felt comfortable that I could do it properly. Once I was comfortable that I could do it I celebrated by buying a new blue tie to add to my collection.

The dressing room was full of characters who were always playing tricks and catching each other out. The aforementioned Andy Rolland was one of the main culprits. He was to catch me out a few times and I recall him having a laugh at my expense over my name. Up until I moved to Dundee, I had always been called James at home. I had a cousin in the Highlands and he was called Jim Oliver and I was always called James to stop us being mixed up. There is a later story about this when I returned to the Highlands but that is for another chapter. I am not sure who had started calling me Jim in the papers but that was what all of the players were calling me. I put up with it for about a week or so and then I made the fateful mistake of trying to correct them. I walked into the 1st team dressing room and someone called me Jim and I said, "My name is actually James, not Jim."

Well, this was the cue for Andy Rolland to start off "Oooh, he said my name is James not Jim". He then addressed the rest of the guys and said, "From now on I must be called Andrew, not Andy." I think that was when I thought to myself, I think I am going to have to get used to being called Jim.

There are still a few people who always call me James and they are my close family and one or two close school friends although to them I am probably better known as my school nickname "JO".

One good thing that came out of it was that my Granny Oliver wrote to me and said that my Granda Jim was delighted to be reading about me being called Jim and she put a £5 note in the letter. I still have that letter somewhere - but the £5 is long gone.

Another episode when I was on the receiving end of a prank (which Andy was part of) was the Chinese Restaurant meal. Andy, Dave Cooper and myself had a couple of beers after training one day and Andy said that he was hungry and asked, "did we want to go for a Chinese sit down?".

We went into a restaurant in the middle of town and ordered our main meals. We had these, then the waiter came and asked if we wanted desserts. Andy said he would have a Knickerbocker Glory, so Dave and I said we would have one each as well. Andy excused himself and went to the toilet and after he was there for a while Davie said he would go and see what is keeping him. When Davie was away the waiter came with the 3 Knickerbocker Glory's. I started on mine and seen Davie coming out of the toilets and walking out the front door. I was wondering where he was going and then it dawned on me that they had done a runner and I was left to pay the bill! I finished my dessert and called over the waiter and said I wanted to pay for my food. He took the bill over for the whole lot. I said that I was only paying for mine and at that point he called his colleagues over and with 5 Chinese waiters surrounding me I had to stump up. They went to take the two other Knickerbockers away but they were told to leave them and I eventually got them finished before leaving the restaurant stuffed. Andy and Davie were not flavour of the month with me that day, but they do say "Never trust a Fifer!"

Davie had a great way of making a few extra pound each week. He would ask the players what LP's they were looking for and he would charge them £3.99 instead of the usual £4.99. What he used to do was go in to the Record Shop area in a shop in town and switch over the price stickers.

Say the latest album was the Eagles at £4.99 he would go and find an old album that had a £2.99 sticker on it and swap them over. He would then take it up to one of the older ladies who ran that part of the shop and they would charge him what was on the sticker. I think Bar Codes were invented to stop Davie. What a character he was and I have some stories about him that could never be put down in writing.

Mrs Clark who was my landlady spoke to me one day and said that she was going to ask the club to find me new digs as she liked having her family over at the weekends. The other players that she had usually went home to their Central Belt homes on Fridays or after the home games on Saturday. Getting up to the Highlands after a game was not possible in those days and there were no Highland clubs in the Scottish Leagues then. I often think how great it would have been to be able to play professional football and still stay at home.

The youngsters in the Highlands nowadays have a great opportunity with ICTFC and Ross County both having professional set ups. Around this time, I was feeling very homesick as I was missing my friends and girlfriend and my mother recalls me being on the phone crying about wanting to come home. It is a very real feeling for youngsters when they are so far away from home for the first time.

Not long after I came to Dundee I was walking along the street when I saw someone familiar walking towards me. This was a lad from Fortrose whom I had played football against in school. I recall our battles on the football pitch and to say he was someone I did not get on with on the football pitch was probably an understatement. However here we were meeting on the street in Dundee and we stopped and spoke to each other asking why we were there.

This was to be the start of a lifelong friendship, although we don't see each other for years at a time, when we do it's like we had met the other day.

Stewart Patience is an imposing figure standing a few inches taller than me and he was down there for University. We arranged to meet up again and he would come to our reserve matches and this turned him in to a United fan which he still is.

He could also get me in to the Students Union where the drinks were much cheaper and many's a Saturday night were spent in the Union bars and then on to one of the many parties at the Students residences. Graeme Payne used to hang about with us and I always think of the sketch of Ronnie Corbett, Ronnie Barker and John Cleese when I think of the 3 of us together.

I ended up getting a digs transfer to Mrs Macallum's in Whitehall Place in the very centre of Dundee. This opened up a whole new world to me at weekends as I was close to all the pubs and nightspots. Not a good place for a party loving Highlander and I was unfortunately going to take advantage of it.

There were two other players staying in these digs and they were Andy Gray and Billy Steele. Billy was from Oakley just outside Dunfermline and had been signed with Rangers but had been released. Andy was of course United's jewel in the crown at this time and was destined to move on to have a brilliant career before going on to fronting Sky Sports. Neither of these guys were strangers to a beer or two.

We all had our own rooms and I managed to get my 8 Track Player and my 8 tracks down from the Highlands and having my music to listen to made the whole place better to be in. I also owned a shotgun and used to go wildfowl shooting in the Highlands before moving to Dundee. Hamish McAlpine and Jackie Copland also had guns and I used to go out with them now and again. Keeping my gun in my room was to become a problem. I was starting to feel at home and I think it was showing in my performances as I was getting a few games and few goals for the reserves.

There was a lot of speculation about a German club coming in for Andy Gray and the deal was just about done. I was sitting in the digs one afternoon when Andy came in to my room and said that's me away and gave me £100 so that the players could have a smoker on his behalf. A smoker was a term for a "piss up" to celebrate a player getting a move. They usually attended it but Andy had been transferred to Aston Villa for £110,000, which was a Scottish record at the time, and had to report to Villa the next day. That was the last time I seen him although I missed him by minutes on a couple of occasions later on. It would be good to catch up some day. Andy's Smoker took place at the hotel just outside Dundee at the roundabout heading off to Perth. I believe it was called Greystanes or something like that back then.

Hamish, Jackie and I decided to go out shooting ducks down at the carse after it. Not a very sensible decision and it ended up with Hamish's long run of consecutive games coming to an end after he fell in to a hole in the dark and I also fell in to the hole and landed on top of him. He damaged his ankle and had to miss out on Saturday's game. He reminded me about this in later years.

Also at the Smoker was the player that United bought to replace Andy. United went out and bought Tom McAdam from Dumbarton and he was the guy who was most drunk at that do. Tom converted from a Centre Forward to be a very good Centre Half and starred for Celtic for a while and I was to bump in to him a few years later at Parkhead.

I was playing regularly for the reserves now and we were told that we had a game on the Friday night against Motherwell. I phoned and told my parents and asked them if they wanted to come and see the game. They had never seen me play in a game of football since I was in primary school and they were really looking forward to it.

I asked Mr McLean if it would be OK for my parents to come to the game and he said that he would arrange tickets for them to watch from a box. The Friday came and I was so excited and met them and got them their tickets. I was sitting in the dressing room fully expecting to play when the Manager read out the team and I was on the bench. I couldn't understand it as I had been playing well and went and asked the Manager why.

Anyone who knows Jim McLean will know that that was probably not the right thing to do as he turned on me. He said that as I am full time, I get a game most Wednesdays against the 1st team and that he wants to see what some of the part-timers can do. I was dropped to let him see what a youngster called Davie Dodds could do.

I think we were winning 4-0 or so at half time and I thought that surely he would put me on but no and the score ended up being 6-0 and with a couple of minutes to go he asked me to get stripped. It broke my heart not being able to play in front of my parents and I could see how disappointed they were to have come all that way just to see me go on the pitch and not even touch the ball. That night I hated Jim McLean.

The following week at training I got a toe injury and I felt it really uncomfortable and could not put any weight on it. I told Andy Dixon the Physio about it and he said that I should try and run it off. I went out on to the track and tried but it was just too painful. The Manager came out and started shouting at me that Andy had told him there was nothing wrong with it and that I was at it. I could hardly walk by this time and eventually they let me stop.

I went down to A&E at Ninewells and they x-rayed my foot and my big toe had a clean break right across it. I took this information back to Tannadice and neither of them apologised to me for making me try to run on it. To say things were not going too well was a bit of an understatement. As I was unable to train, I asked if I could go home for the weekend and I was granted permission.

I had a great weekend at home with my family and caught the Sunday train back to Dundee so that I would be there for Monday morning. The normal ritual on a Monday morning was that all the players would come in and sit in the dressing room catching up with the craic and if the Manager had found out someone had over stepped the mark at the weekend he would come through and pull them out of the dressing room so that they could explain their actions.

I was a regular at getting called in to his office on a Monday morning as I was one of the few guys that stayed over other than local guys. This morning I was sitting quite calm safe in the knowledge that it wouldn't be me this time. Next thing, the dressing room door near came off the hinges and the Manager with his eyes all puffed up, a sure sign that he was raging, looked at me and shouted, "You! Ma office now" as he turned round and headed to his office.

All the guys looked at me and said, "What the hell have you been up to" I shrugged my shoulders and said, "I have no idea".

I walked along to his office and he asked me to shut the door - why I don't know as I am sure people up at Dens Park would have heard him.

He was to utter the phrase that I always remember him saying to me, "What the f*** were you playing at?"

He continued, "I have had that daft old bat of a Landlady of yours on the phone to me saying that you are a bloody terrorist and that she wants you out of the digs right away. She was putting away some ironing for you and found a big bloody gun in your wardrobe and freaked out."

Bear in mind, this was the mid 70's and a couple of weeks prior to that there had been an IRA bomb scare in Boots in Dundee and Mrs Macallum had obviously put two and two together and made five. I explained to the Manager that I went shooting with Hamish and Jackie and that the gun had a gun lock on it and that I had a licence for it. The Manager replied "I bloody hope so, because the police came and took it away".

I had wondered why Mrs Macallum had been so distant with me the night before when I arrived back from the train station, as she usually wanted to know all that was going on. This time she basically opened the door as wide as she needed to hand me a cup of tea and in the morning. It was the same for breakfast.

I had to go to the police station to claim back the gun and after showing them my licence and proof of identity, they handed over my gun. The only problem was it was out of its cover and I would have to walk through the streets of Dundee to get back to the digs. When I pointed this out to the policeman he laughed and said no one would notice. I had to come back for it the next day with my cover. I apologised to the landlady for giving her such a fright but her mind was made up that I was a terrorist and I was on the move again.

The Manager got me digs out at Broughty Ferry with a couple called Eddie and Mhairi Morrison who lived on The Boulevard on the seafront. While I was in that guest house a guy called Stuart Baxter came on trial with United and stayed in the digs. He did not get on with the Manager at all and it was no surprise when he moved on. This was the same Stuart Baxter that in later years was quoted for nearly every Manager's job that was going. He was even mentioned for the Scottish International position a number of times.

It was to be a short term stay there as Eddie and Mhairi were to buy the Invermark Guest House on Monifieth Road. Resident in the Invermark Guest House were some of the other United Players. In it were Jackie Copland, Andy Rolland, Raymond Stewart and I think Tom McAdam. This was to be my last digs in Dundee and they were great.

Raymond Stewart, who was to go on to be a great player for United and Scotland as well as having a great spell with West Ham, was a young lad from around Perth. He stayed through the week and one night he said to me that his girlfriend and her mate were coming through from Perth to see him and did I want to join them. I said I would be delighted to come with him.

Eddie and Mhairi had twin boys and while I was playing football in the garden with them, Raymond lifted one of the big sash windows from the house and shouted to me to say it was time to go and meet the girls. I heard the window slam shut but did not think any more about it. After I finished the game with the lads I came in to a scene of carnage as the window had landed on Raymond's nose and split it right across. We had to phone an ambulance for him as it was bleeding very badly and the towel that Mhairi had put on it was already sodden.

Raymond told me where we were supposed to meet the girls and I went to meet them as he was getting taken away in the ambulance. I had never met his girlfriend or her friend before but thankfully, when I got to where they were due to meet, they were the only two there. I introduced myself as Raymond's pal and tried to tell them that Raymond had been taken away to hospital after the window fell on his nose. They thought I was joking and it took me about 5 minutes to convince them that what I was saying was true. I can't recall how many stitches he got in it but he got no sympathy from the players as they took the mickey out of him.

With Broughty Ferry being quite far out of town from Tannadice I had a problem on Monday mornings when there were no other players in the digs to give me a lift. One of the other players lived out that way and he would give me a lift in on Monday mornings. This player went on to be a real legend at Rangers and helped me in later years by taking a Rangers team to Inverness for a fund raiser for Clachnacuddin FC whom I was then player Manager of. It was none other than Walter Smith.

I remember him picking me up one morning and saying "F**k me Jim, were you out last night? You better get some polos inside you before the Manager smells it".

We would pick up Graeme Payne on the way in. Walter loved playing the Eagles so there was always good music in his car. He and Archie Knox were just starting to take their coaching badges and were starting to do more with the Reserves.

Back when I had been playing against Motherwell for Ross County, their big Centre Half Willie McVie laid me out as I ran on to his elbow. We had a midweek reserve match away to Motherwell and big Willie was playing. I thought to myself he will never remember who I am and I was plotting my revenge. It was a really wet and windy night and the ground conditions were atrocious. I had made a run out wide and the ball was in front of me and Willie was coming to put the ball out for a throw in. I had to slow down to let him get in to a position where I could tackle him. As he slid in, I went in as hard as I could into his leg and body. He got up and just looked at me as if to say, "What the f** was that meant to be?" I had not hurt him at all. I kept out wide for the rest of the game!

Probably the biggest regret I have of my time at United was never getting a game for the first team. I was close to it one day and could probably have made it if I had been asked in different circumstances. On the Wednesday in training Paul Hegarty was taking a turn in goals and I went in for a cross as he came out for it and we clashed heads. I was OK but Paul's eye was gashed wide open. He was currently our 1st team Centre Forward and he was looking really unlikely to be fit for Saturday's derby against Dundee.

On the Thursday night we played Dundee Reserves in a match at Dens Park. I was on the bench for us and we were getting beaten 3-0 early in the second half with goals from amongst others Gordon Strachan and Alec Caldwell. I came on and scored 2 crackers from outside the box against Ally Donaldson to set up a tight finish. I was to come across all 3 of these

Dundee players later in my football life.

What I remember most about that game was in the last minute or so I played a first time 50-yard pass right on to the toe of Billy Steele 10 yards from goal, but he failed to connect properly, and we never got the equaliser. After training the next day the Manager spoke to me in his office in front of John Holt and Paul Sturrock and mentioned my goals and the pass at the end and then asked me if I was up for playing against Dundee on the Saturday.

I should have said "Bloody right, and if I don't score you can fine me a week's wages", however, I knew how desperate Holty and Luggy were to be playing in the first team and I did not want to seem pushy.

I replied with a horrible "Och, I don't know about that".

I suppose that is a Highland trait, that you do not want to be seen to be pushy, whereas the Central Belt guys were much more focussed on getting what they want. Anyway, that is my biggest regret at Tannadice - not taking that chance to play. In the end they played Doug Houston at Centre Forward and as I watched the game, I seen a few crosses that came in which I thought I could have got on to the end of.

It was coming toward the end of Season 75-76 and United were finding it hard going in the league and were flirting with relegation. I had my own worries to contend with as I got news from home that my father's business was going through a hard time and that it was taking its toll on my parents' relationship. I remember taking a call from my mother one Sunday to say that her and my father were splitting up. I went out and walked for miles crying my eyes out. When I got back, I told Mhairi about it and I really did not feel up to training on the Monday.

This really unsettled me and I started feeling as though I needed to be back home. It was getting near the time of the season when decisions were being made about who was getting kept and who was being released. The players used to joke by saying if you want to find out if you are being kept on or not find an old pair of boots and go in and ask if you can get a new pair. If you get the new pair, you are being kept on but if they tell you that these should do you then the writing is on the wall.

I went in and spoke to the Manager and he said that if I would promise him that I would change my ways and become more disciplined he would retain me, however if I could not do that then he would have to release me. I told him that I could not promise him that and that I wanted to go home. I was then released from my contract and I made the preparations to return to the Highlands - but to what, I did not know.

I had a call from Bobby Robson who was the Manager of Ipswich Town asking if I would come down to them for a trial, but I said no to him. I was not interested in playing professional football.

About a month after coming home I had had a few drinks and thought that I would phone Jim McLean and ask if I could come back. The phone rang a few times then I hung up. I was to speak with him about that many years later.

I was about to enter probably the most turbulent time of my life.

My only photo in a United strip. With a young Paul Sturrock.

Chapter 4

Ross County

When I got back home my father and mother had patched things up and were back together again. I was back home and I got a job as a Labourer at WH Mackay's Steelworks. It was the close season, and the Amateur Leagues were starting. I was looking for a game but because I had not been reinstated as an Amateur I was unable to sign for anyone. I trained with the Tain and Balintore guys but was missing actually playing.

My return to the Highlands brought some interest from Ross County who had tried to sign me before I left for United. Ian McNeill had moved on to Wigan Athletic but there were a few at the club who knew of me. The Manager was Jack Lornie but the person who did all the dealing for the club was Morris Newton who was a huge character in the Highland League. The Newton family owned a Bus Company and Garages in Dingwall and were doing very well as the Invergordon Smelter and Nigg Oil Yard were both very busy.

I was asked if I would go and see Morris at his offices in Dingwall and agreed to do so. My father took me there and I went in to the meeting determined not to sign for anything less than £200. We had to wait in Morris' office for him while he dealt with something else.

Next thing he exploded in to the office and said, "Jim, we want you at Ross

County and here is the deal. £500 signing on fee and you can have the choice of any of the Specials on display out front."

The Specials were three cheap cars that were there to entice people in to the showroom. I pointed at the blue Vauxhall Viva HJS 44F and that was the deal done.

As we were waiting for the paperwork to be processed for the football contract and the car Morris asked my father if he played at all. My father astounded me by saying that he had played for Ross County on many occasions. I never said anything at the time but on the way home I said to him, "I did not know that you played for County."

"Och, yes" he said many times in their social club when I was in the band. Morris got the paperwork sorted out I signed and that was me a Ross County player and the owner of my first car. There was however a problem as Morris tried to hand me the key of my new limo. I asked him if he could get it delivered to my house as I was actually banned from driving at the time.

We had a good pre-season and I was feeling very fit and Ross County had a good start to the Season. There were some very good players in the team such as Gordon Seaton, Alan MacLaren, Stan Sokowlowski, Robbie MacKay and a young Richard Campbell who was to become a very well-respected football manager in the Scottish League. I had however started working as a Bouncer on Friday nights at the Disco's in Portmahomack. My cousin Derek was the DJ and my brother George and I were on the door to make sure everyone behaved. I would have a couple of drinks during the night just to keep me going.

One Saturday we were at home to Buckie Thistle and we had a great team display and won 6-0 and I felt I had had my best game of the season so far. I was involved in all the goals and scored 1. On the Monday night at training, I was asked aside by one of the coaches. He told me that someone

Ross County 1976-77
Back Row L to R: Dave Macrae, Stan Sokolowski, Robbie Mackay, Gordon Seaton,
Clive Windsor, Richie Campbell, Tommy Tulloch & John Brankin
Front Row L to R: George Macdonald, Dave Valentine, James Mutch, James Oliver &
Alan MacLaren

had contacted the club to say that I was out on Friday night at the Disco
in Portmahomack and that I was drinking heavily. I explained that I was
working and had only had a couple of drinks. I was however warned that if
it happened again, I would be in big trouble. I explained that I was working
and that I had maybe two pints in around six hours. I asked did he think
I struggled in the game on Saturday and was told that was not the point.
I could not believe it when I was dropped to the bench for the next game
away to Rothes. I was absolutely raging as I sat on the bench and when
I got on in the second half the rage was still inside me. Myself and the
Rothes Centre Half went up for a ball and he pushed me in the back and
the referee blew for a foul. When we were lying on the ground, he gave me
a little rabbit punch and that blew the cork out of the bottle. I got up and
chased him and booted him and was sent off by the referee. As I passed the

Away dug out, I was told to behave by our bench, but I told them to go away f**k themselves.

I walked in to the dressing room and kicked the tray with all the half time tea cups on it and punched a hole in the dressing room door. The Ross County Manager Jack Lornie, who was a lovely guy and very mild mannered came in and asked me to calm down. I told him to go away but not quite in those words.

Needless to say, I got in to quite a bit of bother for this and was given a hefty fine, in fact it was reported in the Ross-shire Journal as the heaviest fine in club history!

When I had calmed down, I apologised to Jack and took my punishment, but I was not feeling good about the Ross County set up at all. It all came to a head a couple of weeks later. We were due to play Fraserburgh at the Broch and I was asked by my mate William Ross from Balintore if I wanted to go down to Aberdeen. It was his Graduation ceremony and I had been at a few Student parties with him when he was in Aberdeen. I told Ross County that I would make my own way to Fraserburgh from there.

The Graduation day went well and we ended up in the Students Union and I was behaving myself with full intentions of getting the bus to Fraserburgh when a couple of young ladies we knew walked in and that was that. We ended up in the Nurses Home until 6.00am and I woke up in Will's flat at around 1.30pm still drunk. I realised that this would be the last straw for Ross County, and I went on an all-mighty bender in the Students Union that day.

I spoke with the Ross County Manager at training on the Monday night and we agreed that it was best if I left the club. By this time, I had got another job at MK Shand Pipe Coating Mill at Saltburn. The shifts there were 5 x 12 hours Mon – Fri and it was difficult to get to training twice a week, so my contract was terminated. Thankfully, I did not have to give the car back and the £500 was well gone.

Looking back on this period, there was a lot of frustration going on and I was taking it out on the football pitch. It was not a good mix.

Chapter 5

Invergordon

The money at MK Shand was very good for a single man living at home and with no football, my Friday nights changed to all out benders which carried on through Saturday and Sunday. I would go out on Friday and return home on Sunday night sometimes not knowing where the hell I had been.

My brother-in-law Will (Chats) Ross was playing for Invergordon FC at the time and he asked me if I wanted a game with them. Will was a brilliant football player and had had trials with Northampton Town as a youngster but he was a home loving type and loved the village life. I suspect my mother or sister were behind Will asking me to see if it would get me out of drinking so much. I started training with them and enjoyed it.

It was great to be getting a game again on a Saturday's as it gave me something to focus on at the weekends. We had a fantastic team at Invergordon under the watchful eye of our manager, the legendary Jock Mackay. Jock always told us about his claim to fame as being the only man to ever score a hat trick of own goals in the one game. He also delighted in telling us about the time he asked his then football manager Sammy Wilson why was he always in the 2nd team to which Sammy replied because we do not have a 3rd team.

I think we only used 14 players all season with a young goalkeeper Bryan Gunn (15) helping us out on one occasion before leaving to play for Aberdeen, Norwich and Scotland. We won 3 cups and the league that year. I was still enjoying a pint or two on a Friday night but could handle it at that age and at that level of football.

The nucleus of that team came from the Balintore area with Willie MacDonald, Alan Stainke, William Ross, Davy John Ross, Richard Hart and myself coming from there. The others were Sammy McClymont (Inver), Tommy Morrison (Tain) and Michael Laird, Dave Valentine, Graham MacKenzie, Christie Reid, Fraser Moir and Gordon Millar from Invergordon.

As a team this was the best unit I ever played in as everyone knew what each other was doing and all the skills and attitudes complimented each other. This team did not really need a manager as we all knew what we had to do.

I played up front on the left and dropped in behind Harty and Graham MacKenzie at times and it was great to have that free role to make things happen and score goals. All three of us ended up with over 20 goals for the season and there were quite a few from the midfielders and the defenders as well. Tommy Morrison, whom I had played with up front at Tain, played right midfield for us and was our Player of the Year after getting in to double figures from that position.

One game I remember quite well was our game away to Bunillidh Thistle. It was more for what happened the night before as opposed to the game itself. There was a dance in Ardgay (just North of Tain) on the Friday night and I was there with some mates. We were having a quiet night and had been in the Lady Ross for a couple of beers.

Next thing a guy started on my mate and the two of them were fighting on the floor. I went to break it up as it was a "handbags at ten paces" sort of fight. All of a sudden someone grabbed me from behind and my jacket was pulled over my head. I spun round and whacked the person who had grabbed me and after I took my jacket off from over my head I looked down and seen a policeman on the floor.

I gave him a hand up, apologising to him as I did so. All in one movement he had my arm up my back and was marching me out of the hall. Outside I was protesting my innocence as he and another policeman handcuffed me and put me in the back of the police car. They left and came back with the guy who had started the fight and he was also cuffed and put in the back of the car beside me.

As we were being driven over to the Police Station in Bonar Bridge the guy beside me started crying and I turned to him and said "Oh, f**king shut up". The two policemen had been speaking to each other and they thought I was speaking to them!

We were taken into the Police station and after giving our details we were thrown into the cells. Despite my protests that I was speaking to the guy who started the trouble they were having none of it. All I will say is that it is hard to keep your balance when you have handcuffs on.

For those of you who do not know, Ardgay and Bonar Bridge are about 14 miles North of Tain on the old A9. Back in those days, there were very little taxis going about and after I was let out of the cells at around 3.00am, I had the prospect of a 21 mile walk home to the villages looming ahead of me. However, when I got out there was Tommy Morrison and his mate who had a car to take me home. My jacket and jersey had both got damaged in the melee and I threw them out of the window of the car on the way home. I got home around 4.00am and crept in to the house quietly. The next day we were heading back up the A9 in the car going to the football and I was telling the lads what happened. Not far outside Ardgay we came round a corner and here was my jersey lying in the middle of the road and around the next corner was my jacket.

When we arrived at Bunillidh's ground at Helmsdale I remember meeting Ally (Bee) Sutherland and he was astonished to see me there as he had been at the dance in Ardgay and thought I may have been in the cells until Monday. I played the whole game and scored our 5th in the last minute, in a 5-2 win.

As the end of the season neared, we were in contention with Alness. They had quite a few Balintore boys in their team as well so there was a good bit of rivalry going on. They had David Skinner (Pinner), Graham Skinner (Coochie), Will Ross, Robert Allan and Willie MacRae in their team. It just shows the strength of players that came from the villages when you look at both teams.

They had finished all their games and were 2 points ahead of us. We still had Muir of Ord and Tain St Duthus to play in Invergordon. Our first game for some reason was moved to a Friday night 7.00pm kick off.

I remember there being a sizeable crowd there and there was a big contingent of the Alness players and their fans there. Muir of Ord were a strong experienced team with a few ex Highland League players and a centre back pairing of Bill Nelson and Billy (Pengy) MacKenzie who were two no nonsense players. Up front they had the very dangerous Donnie Noble and Ronnie Forbes.

I think for the first time that season we were nervous and took some time to settle in to our game. Graham MacKenzie gave us a lead in the first half. We were not playing that great but were restricting Muir of Ord to shooting from long distance. This, however, eventually paid dividends for them as first Ronnie Forbes equalised and then Bill Nelson put them ahead with long range efforts.

With only seconds to go it looked like the best we could manage would be a win in our last game to force a play-off against Alness. We then got a corner on the right and Dave Valentine fired in a beauty and I got a run on Pengy and headed it downwards towards the goals.

Standing almost on the line and in the way of the ball going into the back of the net was Chats but he opened his legs and let the ball go in for a last gasp equaliser! The Invergordon fans and bench erupted and us players were running about like mad men as we knew that the goal had probably won us the league, as Tain St Duthus would be very beatable.

We had a tremendous night in the Marine Hotel and we all realised why it was a Friday night kick off as Jock was wanting us to have 2 nights on the shot.

Our final game of the season was at home to Tain St Duthus and a few of my school pals were playing for them, with my best mate Alan Ross in goals. Alan is the funniest guy I have ever met and I have met some crackers. We grew up with Monty Pythons and whenever we meet, even now, we break in to some of the Python sketches much to the amazement of others in our company. We won the game comfortably 5-0 and with a minute to go we got a free kick 25 yards out and as I hadn't scored this was my chance to finish the game and the season in style.

I fired in a cracker of a right foot shot which fairly fizzed into the net, just for the referee to give offside against my brother-in-law, Chats. If it was nowadays, it would have counted as he was nowhere near the ball and was not interfering with play.

Alan Ross says that he never went for it as he heard the referee blowing for offside. As I said before - Alan is a born comedian. We went back to the Marine where the league win was well and truly celebrated.

We still had our end of season trip to go and this year it was down to Fort William. Football teams end of season trips are notoriously funny weekends away when everyone lets their hair down.

Graham MacKenzie was unable to make it this year but we called upon a

Invergordon - North of Scotland Reserve Champions 1976-77
Back Row L to R: Michael Laird, William Ross, Graham MacKenzie, Willie MacDonald, Dave Valentine, David Ross, Alan Stainke & James Oliver
Front Row L to R: Fraser Moir, Richard Hart, Sammy McClymont, Jock Mackay (Manager), Christie Reid, Gordy Millar & Tommy Morrison

Below: Celebrations in the Marine Hotel for Invergordon FC

friend who was up from Dundee to make up the numbers. Graeme Payne was up for a wee holiday and he came with us. We travelled down on the Saturday morning and we booked in to our hotel. We made our way to Laggan Park the home of Fort William FC at the foot of Ben Nevis.

At this stage Fort William were applying to get in to the North Caledonian League and a lot of their better players were still playing shinty. Graeme Payne was playing for us and was obviously standing out when one of the Fort Officials approached Jock and said who is that number 9 and Jock replied that it was Graham Makenzie. The Fort official who must have known Graham Mackenzie said "that's not Graham MacKenzie as he is about 5' 11" and 13 stone" and Jock came out with the classic line "Aye but he's not been keeping well".

It was an unofficial friendly so it was not like the they were going to complain about it but if Jim McLean had found out about it then Graeme would have been in trouble. I am surprised he did not find out about it as he seemed to have his spies everywhere.

We had a few beers with the Fort William guys and then went back to the Hotel. It was quite a long night and I remember myself and Dornoch (one of the supporters) got locked out of the hotel. I had to climb up the fire escape and eventually managed to get in. This was not to be my last attempt at climbing buildings and going in windows. The next morning, we all met for breakfast and tried to piece the night together before checking out and jumping on the bus.

Just as we were on the outskirts of Fort William, I realised that I did not have my wallet. I remembered it falling off the bed when I had got in and thought it must be on the floor at the far side of the bed. They turned the bus around and I went back in to the hotel and found the wallet where I thought it might be.

As I was handing the key back in to the receptionist, she said to me, "By the way, there will be a charge being sent to the club for a soiled mattress in Room 74."

Armed with this vital piece of information, I bounded back on to the bus and said that I had found it and "By the way, who was it that was in Room 74?"

Thinking that something of value had been found in it the Occupier of that room shot his arm up in the air and shouted with glee "That's me".

"Well, there will be a charge being sent to the club as you have pished the bed." I said.

I shall spare the blushes of the person involved.

After the stay in the Bonar Bridge police station, I was given a summons to appear at Dornoch Sherriff Court on a charge of police assault. On the day of the trial, my mother drove me up to the court and we were sitting in the court as the other people ahead of me were up in front of Sherriff Stewart who had quite reputation for being very strict. The guy that was up in front of me was being charged with being on a motorcycle without wearing a helmet. The Sherriff asked him if he could give him an explanation as to why he was on the motorcycle without the helmet and he replied, "I was drunk". I burst out laughing at this admission and Sherriff Stewart gave me the death-ray stare.

My case was up next and to say that the policeman had embellished his story would be an understatement. He described a scene of an all-out attack on the police by myself and that I continued to struggle and shout obscenities to them in the police car. Once detained at the police station, I continued to struggle with them, and they had to calm me down.

Sherriff Stewart said to me that my behaviour was shocking and asked if I have anything to say in my defence. I said that what the policeman had said was not accurate.

He then said to me, "Are you calling the Constable a liar?"

I said that I did not recognise his recollection as being what happened but that I apologise if that was what happened. I was charged with police assault and fined £70.

The fine had to be paid there and then or I would be put in custody until it was paid. Luckily my mother had the money on her and I managed to stay out of the cells. I was so disappointed by the evidence that the police officer had given as it was certainly not what occurred.

With the football season now over, it was back to late Friday nights and boozy weekends. Arriving home late from Balintore pub one Saturday night I found that there was nothing substantial to eat in the fridge.

Feeling hungry I decided to drive in to Tain to get some Chips from the late-night takeaway that parked on the High Street. This was not a good idea as I had been drinking all day. In those days I was driving a Mini, when Minis were Minis, and after having my chips - I nearly had my chips - as I was involved in a collision.

Just outside Tain, I came round a corner and drove into the back of a Volvo estate which was stopped at the side of the road. Mini v Volvo is not a good match up and how I survived that crash I will never know. I remember coming to as they were putting me in to the ambulance but then blacked out again. I woke up the next day in hospital in Inverness. As I was lying in hospital, I thought to myself that I have to get away from the Highlands as I am going completely off the rails.

Both my knees were damaged and I had several cuts on my hands and forehead and a huge bruise on my chest the shape of a steering wheel. I was told that I was found lying on top of the engine and had come through the windscreen. I found what was left of my car a few years later in a dump and I can't believe how I managed to get out the window. I could now understand how my chest was so bruised, as the steering wheel was also out of the windscreen with the whole steering column bent.

It was time to get my life back on track and I made the decision to leave the Highlands and move to Aberdeen where my girlfriend was in College.

Chapter 6

Moving to Aberdeen / Rosslyn Sports

As I lay in hospital in Inverness, I made up my mind that I was going to go down to Aberdeen and see if I could get a job there.

I had a girlfriend who was at college in Aberdeen and I had somewhere to stay for a couple of nights while I looked for a job and a place to stay. I got home and told my parents what I was going to do and I think they were quite relieved that I was going to try and do something positive. They said that they would help me as much as they could.

When I was travelling down to Aberdeen on the train, I was reading the P&J and was looking through the jobs section. There was a job advertised for Structural Engineering Technicians and the company was called Derick Sampson & Partners (Structural & Consulting Engineers). In school my favourite classes were my Engineering Science and Engineering Drawing and I felt that this job was perfect for me.

Their offices were on the 3rd Floor of an old office block on Union Street quite near the Music Hall. I went straight from the station to their offices and this took me ages as my knees were very sore and I had to stop a few times. When I got to the bottom of their stairs I nearly cried as they were on the 3rd floor. When I got up to the 3rd floor and opened their door there was another flight of stairs up to their reception. I had to carry my bag with me as well as there was nowhere to leave it.

I spoke to the receptionist (Helen) and I said that I would like an application form for the position that they were advertising. I was given the form and asked if I could fill it in there and then and was allowed to do this. At this point the boss came in to the office and I remember thinking how much energy this guy had.

His name was Tom White and he was the senior partner in Aberdeen. I was introduced to him and when I finished my application I asked when they would be making a decision. I was told they would let me know on Wednesday if I was being called for an interview. With no contact number in Aberdeen, they asked me to call back on Wednesday. I left and made my way to where my girlfriend stayed in Ashvale Place which was not too far from Union Street but was still a bit of a trek in my current state.

On Wednesday I went back to Derick Sampson & Partners and climbed the stairs again. The good news was that they were going to give me an interview and could I come back on Friday. This was the best news I could have had and it made the descent of the stairs and walk back to Ashvale Place feel so much easier.

My girlfriend's flatmate's boyfriend was playing for Aberdeen and I had met them before when I had come up for Dundee United reserve games and also for weekends. His name was George (Pele) Campbell and he came from Fort William. George is now out in Melbourne and through the wonders of Facebook we are back in touch. George and his two pals who also played for Aberdeen Jim Rodger and John Gardiner were sharing a flat and there was a spare bed in it. If I was successful with the interview there was a place for me to stay.

On Friday I was ready for my first interview but I did not know what to expect as the jobs I had got before were my one at Dundee United where the interview consisted of playing football and my other jobs were through word of mouth or who you knew. Also, as I had not much clothes with me, I think they seen me in the same clothes for the 3 times I was in their offices.

Anyway, the climb up the stairs was getting easier and I was getting used to meeting Helen who was always cheery. I sat for a while and then I got called in to Tom's office. He was reading my Application Form and I think it was the first time he had looked at it. He started asking me questions about Engineering which were way ahead of what I had studied in school. He said to me "You are a Structural Technician, aren't you?"

"No," I replied, "but I seen that you were looking for at least two and I thought maybe you would take on an Apprentice as well?"

He looked at me and said, "I hadn't thought about that."

He spoke to me for a little while longer and I told him about my Engineering subjects in school and about my father and both my grandfathers being steeped in the Construction Industry.

On my application form I had put down that I had a spell at W H Mackay's and he said to me that they had done some work with them in the past. He asked me if I would come back in on the Monday and he would let me know then.

It felt like a really long weekend until I had to climb the stairs again. I had not applied for anything else and I was so desperate to be given this opportunity. When I got up the stairs Helen gave me a smile and I thought to myself I think she knows something. Tom asked me to come through and he said the words I so wanted to hear.

"We would like to offer you an apprenticeship as a Structural Engineering Technician"

I was absolutely delighted. I found out later on that he had phoned Graham Mackay, the owner of W H Mackays, to ask about me and what my background was like. God knows what Graham told him but it seemed to do the trick. The fact that Graham was one of my father's best friends and my father had done him a few favours when he was starting up W H Mackay's would have helped. It just seemed like this was meant to be for me.

I started on £20 per week and my digs were £14, so I did not have much spare cash. I phoned and told my parents the good news and they were delighted and they sent me some money to keep me going. I was to get used to what I would call the Red Cross Parcel delivery every now and again.

I moved in with George, Jim and John while I found my feet in Aberdeen. Gradually my knees were getting better and I was starting to be able to jog and although my knees kept swelling up the pain was not so bad.

One of the Structural Engineers in the Derick Sampsons, Steve Booth, used to go swimming every Sunday down at Aberdeen Beach. Before they went in for a dip, they used to have a game of football on the grass in front of Codonas.

About 3 months after going to Aberdeen I felt as though I could play a game with them. This started to be a regular event for me except for the swimming and I was soon aiming my sights a bit higher for a game. I had been reading in the paper about a team called Banks o' Dee who were the top Junior team in Aberdeen and I thought that I would go and watch them play.

I got on a bus in town one Saturday which was going up to Altens and I seen a guy who had a sports bag and I asked him if he could tell me where to get off for the Banks o' Dee pitch as I was going to watch their match. It turned out that he was their goalkeeper and I think his name was Mike Stephen.

I watched the game and I thought to myself that I could play at that level so when the game ended, I asked to speak to one of their officials. I asked if I could come along to their training and he said that they have training every Sunday at Inverdee. I turned up at Inverdee the next day and it was all kids of about 15. As a 19-year-old I stuck out quite a bit. I came along for 3 weeks and nobody from the club spoke to me or asked me if I wanted to go and train with their 1st team. I just felt that there was an arrogance about the whole place and it pissed me off.

After this let down, I went back to playing on a Sunday in front of Codonas. By this time I had met some lads from back home and we all moved in to a flat in Lilybank Road near the Northern Hotel. Just before I left the flat in Constitution Street, I nearly ended the career and baby making abilities of one of the Aberdeen 1st team players.

I was sound asleep in the flat when George and Jim came in to our room and said that there was someone trying to get in the kitchen window. I got up and went through and here is this big shadowy figure trying to get in the top window. He had one leg in, and was trying to get the other in when I grabbed his leg and started pulling. He started shouting as his crown jewels were getting crushed, "Stop it, for f**k's sake, it's me - Joe!"
I said, "Who the f**k's Joe?"
The others told me it was Joe Smith. I let him go and he came in. I think he had been out and was looking for somewhere to stay as he could not get in his own house.

My two flatmates in Lilybank Place were John Browning from Balintore and Alec MacLeod from Tain. In the flat above us was a transvestite and in the other flat in the block was Buckie Jim. We were there for a couple of months and the landlady asked us to move as we almost burnt the whole building down trying to cook one night.

We had been living off Chip Shops and Takeaway meals but we were now looking for something more wholesome. My mother is a fantastic cook, and I was craving some of her home-made broth.

I phoned her and asked her how to make it. She told me to get a bone from the butchers (you were allowed to do this then) and put it in a pan of water, chop up some carrot, onion & turnip add a little salt and bring it to the boil and leave it simmering for 30 minutes.

We got all the ingredients and set to the task. It was bubbling away in the pan and we set our watch. The Northern Hotel was 5 mins walk from us so we went down there for a couple of pints while we waited for the soup to be ready.

As we walked back up the street we could smell burning and when we opened the bottom door to the flat the smoke started billowing out. We made it up the stair to find the remnants of the bone and the veg welded black to the bottom of the pan.

I called my mother and told her what had happened and she said did you leave it simmering or leave it boiling…I suppose when I asked her what does simmering mean she worked out what we had done wrong. On top of a wasted meal, we had to by a new soup pan for the Landlady.

I found a flat in King Street above what was then the Jubilee Bar but was to become the East Neuk. However, the owner of the flat, who also owned the pub, required a Company Let. I spoke to Tom White about it and he agreed to help and Derick Sampsons took on the let and I had to pay it each month to Helen. John and Alec moved with me and it was a two bedroomed flat and was to become my home and the home of several other lads from the Highlands over the next few years. This flat was to become party central!!

I was needing to get back to playing football and I was speaking to my fellow Apprentice Ian Corsie. Ian was a year younger than me but was a year ahead of me in our Apprenticeships and he asked me what I had been doing when I left school. I told him that I had been signed as a Professional Footballer with Dundee United and he said are you playing for anyone now to which I replied "No, but I would love a game."

Ian's father worked with a lad called Ronnie Clark who ran a football team, to which he said, "Do you want me to ask?"

"Yes please." I said.

Ian's dad Harry worked in the SMT Garage just off Union Street almost across the road from where we worked. Ian said that Ronnie would like to speak to me and we went across one lunch time to see him. Ronnie said that his team Rosslyn Sports had a cup final that weekend and that he could not put me in for that but that he would arrange for me to play for a team on Saturday so that he could have a look. I think the name of the team I played for on the Saturday up at Hazlehead were ALC Gunners and they were in the 7th Division Amateur in Aberdeen football. I don't think there is anything lower.

I must have done well as Ronnie asked me to come along to the cup final the next day and listed me as a sub. It was strange going in to a dressing room and not having met anyone before and to be listed as a sub in a cup final as well. The game was up at Heatheryfold and was against Rosslyn's arch rivals Woodacon. I recognised one of the Woodacon players as he was Dougie McIldowie from Invergordon. Anyway, we won the game 3-2 after extra time and that was quite a first game to have in Aberdeen.

Most of the games for Rosslyn were through the week as they were in the Welfare League and we had the odd game at the weekends if we were playing in the East of Scotland Cup. We did try to have training sessions once a week and it was great meeting other people and widening my circle of friends in Aberdeen. I have kept in touch with John Foote and we meet up every few years for a meal and a few drinks with our wives.

It was great to meet with them for a beer and I also had my student pals as I was enrolled by Derick Sampson & Partners to do an ONC Course in Building Construction at Aberdeen Technical College. Here I met up with another lifelong friend Steve Cook. Steve and I hit it off right away and Thursday afternoons after college usually ended up with us being in the Students Union all night.

Rosslyn were going quite well in the league but Woodacon were too far ahead of us for us to catch them. We were drawn against Broughty Ferry from Dundee who were the favourites to win the East of Scotland Cup but we beat them over two legs with the second leg in Dundee being quite tasty. They were trying to get in to our dressing room at the end. We were OK though as we had some hardy buggers in our team that new how to look after themselves and they probably dodged a bullet by not getting in. The final was against Letham from Perth. The first leg was played at Linksfield Stadium and we won it comprehensively 5-1 and we drew the return leg in Perth 2-2 with a great display.

That was the game where I introduced my perm to the world. It was 1978 and half the Scotland World Cup team had tight curly perms. I did not want a tight curly perm as I was after the shaggy perm that was used by the likes of Fleetwood Mac.

I went down to Ricky Simpson's Hair Salon near the Students Union on the Friday afternoon and asked for a Shaggy Perm and explicitly said that I did not want any curls. Simpson's was well known for having lots of gorgeous hairdressers and my day got off to a bad start when I was shown to a seat by the only bloke in the shop.

I once more said that I was looking for a Shaggy Perm and that I did not want curls. He nodded and got to work with the various solutions etc. Then he put me under a large heater type thing which went right over my head and then he left me presumably to cook.

I thought that he seemed to be a way for a while and I was feeling it quite hard to turn my head. Next thing he appears with a look of horror on his face as he had obviously forgotten about me.

I will never ever forget what happened next as he switched of the "Perm Cooker" and started to try and get me out of it. As he raised the heater the curls started coming out from under the edge and the more, he took it off the worse it was getting. Eventually the whole thing was off and I looked like one of them Dandelion's that you blow the seeds off.

I just looked in stunned amazement at ball of curled up hair that was surrounding my head.

"Which part of I don't want any fucking curls didn't you understand?" I said as he looked petrified.

I could hear the girls all sniggering. I said there is no way that I am paying for this and he agreed as I stormed out of the salon.

I could feel the wind drag in it as I walked back to the flat in King Street. I had a shower to see if that would help but that made it even worse as the curls got even tighter. The worst thing was it was lunchtime and I had to go back to work!!

I walked back up Union Street absolutely sick and worried that people might see me. I got in to the building and walked up the stairs. It felt harder to walk up the stairs with the perm than it did with two dodgy knees. As I got to the last section, I got half way up the stairs and then Helen could see my head. She looked in amazement before absolutely creasing herself in laughter and I said "I like it as it is all the style for footballers just now" on the outside I was trying to pretend I was pleased with it but inside I was dying.

I then had to confront the Engineers and once they had recovered their composure, they were merciless in the stick they were handing out. All the time I was pretending that I liked it while inside I was dying.

When I turned up for the football the next day the players were 10 times worse with their comments but a headed goal in the final helped me. The players were saying all they had to do was aim for the ball of hair and Jim would be thereabout.

I had really enjoyed my half season with Rosslyn and had scored over 20 goals in that time. It was great to be back playing again.

We had a great end of season night out and I consoled myself in the knowledge that I could never again have such a bad hairstyle. It took about 3 months to grow out.

The rest of the Scottish Perms were to descend upon Argentina when Ally MacLeod had us all believing that we were going out there just to pick up the trophy. We were all caught up in World Cup fever as our first game against Peru approached. It was going to be a win against them and then a win against the minnows in the group Iran and then a play-off with the Dutch to see who the Group Winners would be. Peru however had not been delivered the script and as their 3rd goal went in, we heard an almighty crash outside our flat on King Street. We looked out the window and here were the remains of a TV that had been launched out the window of the flat 2 stories above us. It was back in the days when Radio Rentals had started hiring out TV's and the guys in that flat above had hired one for the World Cup. They were in court for it later on that year and got a hefty fine and had to pay for the TV.

Archie Gemmill scored the goal of the tournament against the Dutch as Scotland restored some pride. I remember meeting him at a football do and telling him what I was doing as he scored. He said that many people had told him what they were doing or where they were when he scored but that my story was by far the best.

Our trip back from the East of Scotland Cup Final in Perth was epic and far too many things happened that can't be written down. Suffice to say there was a lot of drink involved.

After the end of the season Ronnie Clark asked to meet me one lunch time and he said to me that he had been contacted by Fraserburgh and Arbroath who were both interested in signing me.

I spoke with Tommy MacMillan who was the new Fraserburgh Manager and I really liked him. He told me about his plans for Fraserburgh and he wanted me to be part of it. Tommy was a former Aberdeen centre half and I was happy to sign for him.

Rosslyn got the princely sum of £100 for me.

Above: Rosslyn Sport - East of Scotland Juvenile champions 1977-78
Back Row L to R: Ron Clark (manager), Alan Anderson, Neil Shepherd, James Oliver, Donald Cordiner, Ian Keith, Gordon Cairns & George Spencer (trainer)
Front Row L to R: John Foote, Stuart Davidson, Graham Davidson, Gary Miller, Derek Milne, Bob Young, Alan Low & Dave Coull

Right: Me with the East of Scotland Juvenile Cup.

Chapter 7

Fraserburgh

I had never been to Fraserburgh before having missed my bus there when at Ross County. Fraserburgh is called "the Broch" and we were to start our pre-season training there. Tommy MacMillan and his assistant Ian Wilson who had played at Aberdeen with him had recruited some other players from Aberdeen and we were to travel up to Fraserburgh in a couple of cars. The other players were Billy Mitchell, Ronnie MacDonald, Jimmy Smith and Willie Donald.

As we arrived at the Bellslea we were introduced to the local lads and I was incredibly nervous as I was frightened for the first time that I might be out of my depth. We were out on the pitch for our first session and it was strange not actually knowing anyone. The only one I had seen before was Billy Mitchell as he had bright red hair and I seen him playing in Amateur football in Aberdeen but I had never spoken to him. Then this lad came up to me and said "Do you remember me?" I had to say to him that I didn't. He introduced himself as Alfie Smith who had been down at Dundee United on trial when he played for Peterhead. I did remember that there were 3 Peterhead players on trial and Jim McLean asked me to look after them as I was a Highlander.

Bruce Buchan, who was one of the trainers at the time, says he will never forget the first thing he seen me doing that day and from that moment he knew I would do well. As we stepped out on to the park there was a ball lying there and I took a shot from the half way line which thumped off the bar. He told me this years later and I recall doing it and it was due to me being nervous that made me want to put the ball in the net to give myself confidence.

We had a good pre-season and I got to know some of the great local characters that played for the Broch. Kenny Rodgers, John Duthie (Tosie), Bertie Bowie, Dave Mackenzie and Jim Crawford were local lads who were Brochers through and through. It was good fun playing and training there and I looked forward to going to training twice a week and to our games on the Saturday. I enjoyed the crack so much with the Fraserburgh boys that I was soon staying up on the Saturday night and getting a bus back to Aberdeen on the Sunday. Sometimes if we had a really good weekend, I would get a lift back to Aberdeen with Jim Crawford on a Monday morning.

Tommy MacMillan was a Taxi Driver in Aberdeen and he would have done a 12-hour shift before picking us up in his taxi to go to training. Most of the guys would have a snooze in the back of the car on the way to training and the person in the front was left to speak to Tommy. As I was last to be picked up on King Street the others had grabbed the back seats by the time I was picked up. One night as I was sitting in the front seat of the car, I felt the car drifting out into the middle of the road and I looked over and seen that Tommy's eyes were closed. I started speaking to him and he opened his eyes and got us back on the right side of the road. I talked non-stop until we got to Fraserburgh. I even woke the guys in the back, much to their annoyance, so that we could get a good conversation going. At least it kept Tommy awake.

All was going well and I was getting more and more confidence and I was enjoying the training that we were getting from Tommy and Ian. We had a great win away to Fort William in the Scottish Qualifying Cup where I scored our 4th goal and the Manager said in the paper that I would soon make a return back to the Scottish League if I continued playing as I was. Everything was going great then there was a fall out between the Manager and John Duthie which ended up in John being suspended.

The Fraserburgh Committee decided to back the player and this left Tommy in an untenable position. Tommy resigned as Manager and his assistant Ian Wilson went with him. I wondered where this was going to leave us lads from Aberdeen as Tommy had taken us there.

The new Manager was a Fraserburgh legend Bobby Forsyth. I had a problem with Bobby right away as I could not make out a word he was saying. Bobby had a very broad Doric accent and I usually just nodded my head when he was speaking to me. He was also cross eyed which did not help.

When the team was announced I used to get changed quickly and get out on the pitch to get some shots at goal to get the confidence going. The team got named and I was playing No.9 so I got changed as Bobby was talking away in the background.

Once I was changed, I grabbed a ball, went to go out and Bobby grabbed me and said, "Far are ye gawn? Am spikin' to you!"

I had not been listening as I thought he had been speaking to someone else! I think that Bobby was to blame for me having a hat-trick stolen off me at Lossiemouth. I usually played number 10 if I could but this day, I was given the number 9 shirt as Jim Crawford had been given the number 10 the week before when I was injured. There was a mix up on the team sheet as I scored my first ever Highland League hat-trick that day and could not wait to get back to Aberdeen to get a Green Final and read all about it. Imagine my disappointment on opening the paper to read about Jim Crawford's superb hat trick in a 3-0 Fraserburgh win!

We were a decent footballing team and were more than capable of beating any of the top teams on our day. We finished mid table and had a strong finish to the league. The Buchan Derbies were the big games for the Broch and no doubt Peterhead fans. There was an intense rivalry between the teams and at this time Peterhead had had the upper hand in the recent games.

They were riding high in the league and were pushing for a possible title surge when they arrived at Bellslea looking for a win to keep their title charge going. We battled out a 2-2 draw with them that day and that was the first time I seen a lad called Charlie Duncan play. He was everywhere for Peterhead that day. He was to become a team mate of mine in later years at Inverness Thistle and was undoubtedly the best player I played with in the Highland League. He was also to become a Fraserburgh legend as he played and managed them for many years.

It was great to see the Broch fans delighted at putting a spoke in the Blue Toon's title push and I was delighted to get our first goal that day. It was to be quite a significant goal for me as I was being watched by Montrose FC that night. Their manager, Bobby Livingstone was there with his father and when I scored with a header from a corner while outjumping a 6' 5" centre half and a 6' 4" goalkeeper, his father turned to Bobby and said, "Sign him."

A few weeks later we were drawn against Peterhead in the Bells Cup Quarter Final, again at Bellslea. This was our last chance of any silverware that season and it did not look good as we fell behind to a Charlie Duncan goal mid-way through the second half. I managed to grab us an equaliser with a shot from outside the box in to the bottom corner that the goalie never even moved for. Billy Mitchell then popped up with a winner to send the Bellslea faithful home delighted and the team in to a home semi-final against Keith FC.

I don't remember much about the Keith semi-final other than I think it was on a Sunday and we won 1-0 and I think Bertie Bowie scored to take us through to the final against Buckie.

We played Buckie in the Final at Bellslea on the following Thursday night. It seemed strange to play a Cup Final on your own home pitch but we were certainly not complaining. I gave us an early lead but two goals from Malcolm Cowie either side of half time gave Buckie the lead. I scored my second to level the scores and take us in to extra time. An amazing 3 goals in the first 10 minutes of extra time put us in the driving seat to lift the trophy. Bertie Bowie who was probably the fastest player I ever played with scored our 3rd then I completed my hat trick and Willie Donald scored another 2 to give a final score line of 6-2. With it being a Thursday night and us having won a cup there was no chance of me going back to Aberdeen that night and I ended up being there until the Sunday. The Brochers certainly knew how to party.

I had stayed overnight in Fraserburgh on quite a number of times and in the main they were usually just great nights with plenty of booze and lots of partying. I recall one night being in a party when I found the Meatloaf album Bat out of Hell. The guys had not heard it before so I introduced them to it in particular the intro to "You took the words right out of my mouth" where they say "On a Hot Summers night would you offer your throat to the Wolf with the red roses?" This album soon became a favourite with the guys.

Some nights I would stay with John Duthie and sometimes it would be Bertie Bowie. I was responsible for Bertie meeting up with his wife Denise. I was staying at Bertie's that weekend and we had been at a dance or disco in the town somewhere and I took a young lady back to Bertie's for a party. Once I got back there, I fell asleep and when I woke up the next day, I asked Bertie who was the young lady that I had taken back to the party

Above: Fraserburgh F.C. - Bells Cup winners 1978-79
Back Row L to R: Willie Donald, James Oliver, Bobby Forsyth, George Malley
(trainer) & Dave Mackenzie
Middle Row L to R: Eddie Gammack, Kenny Rodgers, Sponsor, Bertie Bowie & Alfie
Smith
Front Row L to R: Bruce Buchan (trainer), Billy Mitchell, Tommy MacQuire, John
Duthie & Jim Crawford

and what had happened to her. He told me that when I fell asleep, he had given her a coffee and walked her home. Several years later I find out that he started going out with her after that night and he then married her!! Cilla Black had nothing on me!!

Just before I left Fraserburgh I unfortunately got involved in some trouble out at the dance hall at Rosehearty. I was with a group of players and fans and we had left Fraserburgh to go to the Dance in Rosehearty Hall. As we were walking in the door one of the bouncers said to me "Sorry Mate you have had too much to drink". I know that on this occasion I had not had too much and as the others were trying to plead my case, I said to them that it was okay, and I would sit outside for a while and try and get in later. I was sitting there and four young lads dressed in leathers came up to the door and started banging on it. The bouncer opened the door had one look at them and told them that they were not getting in. A scuffle started between them and they pulled the bouncer out the door. I thought to myself that if I helped the bouncer then he would let me in.

I started pulling the guys off the bouncer who then leapt to his feet ran in the door and shut it. That left me on my own outside looking at these four guys who were probably about 16 or17 year old. I tried to reason with them that I was only trying to stop the fight but I could see that they were going to attack me. I remember connecting with one guy's chin and another guy's nose before the doors opened and the bouncers and a few of the Broch players came out and chased them away. We all went inside and I did not think any more about it.

A few days later I was sitting in the flat in Aberdeen and there was a knock at the door and it was the police. They wanted to speak to me about an incident that happened at a dance at Rosehearty. One of the guys had suffered a broken jaw and his parents were looking for me to be charged with assault. I could not believe it as if I had not tried to defend myself, I could have been the one who was injured. The charge was that I used excessive force in defending myself. I had this hanging over me for a few months and then I got the letter from the Court to attend a trial at Banff Sherrif Court.

By this time, I was at Montrose FC and it was on a day when we were training. I had to get a bus up from Aberdeen to Banff and when I got to the Court they asked me who was representing me. I had to ask what that meant. I was told that I should have a lawyer to represent me and if I did not have one, I would have to represent myself. I was shitting myself - a trained lawyer, I was not.

When the trial started the charge was read out and I was asked how I plead and I said Not Guilty. The four lads whom I had met that night at Rosehearty were there and the lad with the broken jaw was asked to give evidence and he could hardly speak. I was asked if I wanted to ask him any questions. I just said "Who was it that started the trouble?" The story came out and the judge said that I should not be charged with assault but that all five of us should be charged with Breach of the Peace.

I received a £60 fine and left the court house. I had to wait an hour for the next bus to Aberdeen and decided to pop in to a pub near the Court House for something to eat. I walked in there and the 4 lads were playing pool. I spoke to them and said I was sorry for what had happened and they were OK with it and claimed that it was their parents that were pushing for the charges to be placed.

At the end of that season the top eleven teams in the Highland League were invited to take part in the Access 5 a side tournament which was held at Aviemore. This was a fantastic occasion held over a weekend. The Highland League teams were joined by invited clubs from the Scottish League and Rangers, Celtic, Hibs and St Johnstone were amongst those that had entered teams.

In total there were 16 teams I think and there were group games to begin with and we were drawn in the same group as Highland League Champions Keith, Deveronvale and Celtic. In our first game we had to play a very strong Keith team and we got beat 3-2. We seen this game as pivotal to us progressing as we were both expected to beat Deveronvale and that Celtic would win the group.

We felt a bit down and had a couple of beers after the game as we had to wait a few hours to play Deveronvale. I think Deveronvale must have beaten Celtic as that opened the door again for us and even though we had had a few beers we managed to beat them 2-1. With Keith also beating Celtic that left the group with Keith on top with 4 points and Deveronvale and ourselves on 2 points and Celtic with no points. Keith, who were already through, were to play Deveronvale and we were to play Celtic. All we had to do was beat Celtic to qualify and it was the first game scheduled for the Sunday morning!! I would imagine the Celtic players were tucked up in their beds early. The Broch boys however were there to party and party we did.

It was a fantastic night as friends and foes from the different clubs all got in the party mood and the Aviemore Centre bars must have done a roaring trade that night. I managed to get my hands on one of the big promotional Access Cards and was attempting to buy drinks with it all night with no success.

We were staying in the Chalets in the centre and there were some outdoor trampolines just outside our chalet and on the pathway to all the other chalets. Myself and Jim Blacklaw of Elgin City decided it would be fun to bounce around naked on the trampolines at around 3.00am in the morning. The Highland League people were not the only residents of the chalets and there were plenty of other tourists enjoying the spectacle. Then we seen two couples coming along and it was Jock MacDonald (Inverness Thistle Chairman) and his wife and Jock Stein (Scottish International Manager) and his wife and they had a good laugh at what was going on or had a good laugh at something else!

Following on from that shenanigans somebody thought that it would be a good idea to lift a Mini and put it sitting on a wall. I have no idea who was involved but several Fraserburgh and Peterhead players will be glad that no finger prints were taken! The reaction from the owner when they came to retrieve their car was priceless. This was viewed from our balcony around 6.00am and we were due to take on the mighty Celtic in a few hours.

It was time to go to bed and I was in one of the top bunks. Billy Urquhart from Inverness Caley had been locked out of his Chalet by his team mates and he asked if he could sleep on our floor. As I was trying to get up the ladder to my bunk I slipped and landed on Billy lying on the floor. How that never ended his career I will never know. Billy and I were to meet up again at Wigan Athletic where we were to have other adventures off the park.

I recall that I was still very drunk when the game started against Celtic and I never made the starting 5. It was a close game but we were holding our own. I would imagine the young Celtic players were getting drunker by the minute with the fumes coming from the Brochers.

One of our boys was needing off to be sick and I was told to go on. The subs were "rolling" as one came off another just went on in their place over the side of the ice rink. As I attempted to go over the side of the ice rink wall I fell in a heap on the floor. Not a good look and as I was getting back to my feet, I could see Jock MacDonald and Jock Stein looking and pissing themselves laughing as Jock MacDonald had obviously told Jock that I was one of the Trampoline Double Act.

I did however manage to score a goal in a 4-3 defeat which we thought was a decent enough score in the circumstances and a good way to end the tournament. However, Keith beat Deveronvale leaving ourselves, Celtic and Vale with two points and it was ourselves who qualified as we had scored the most goals out of the 3 teams on 2 points.

By the time we realised that we were still in the tournament we were back on the booze and our Quarter Final game against I think St Johnstone or it may have been Coventry City ended up in a 5-1 doing. I blame the manager for not even putting me on for that game!!

What a fantastic weekend that was as the camaraderie of the people who represented the Highland League was so evident. It is without doubt the best league I was ever involved in for crack. There is now a Facebook page called Highland League Legends and the Access 5 A-Sides are quite often mentioned.

The last thing for me to do at Fraserburgh was to be a guest in the Bertie Bowie Testimonial Match against Aberdeen. Bertie was a huge favourite with the Broch fans and there was a big turnout for the game against a strong Dons line up which included Leighton, Dornan, McMaster, McLelland, McLeish, Cooper, Bell and Davidson. Young Dave Robertson opened the scoring for Fraserburgh before John McMaster equalised.

I remember watching McMaster playing for Aberdeen and he was one of the most gifted players I have ever seen. What an awareness he had for the game and his first time passing was sublime.

I came on at half time when it was 1-1 and put the Broch ahead after 62 minutes. I skinned Alex McLeish on the half way line and held off Dougie Bell before slipping it through Jim Leighton's legs.

I remember reading Jim talking in the Sunday Mail about being bandy but that nobody had nutmegged him to score. Someone at the game caught me on camera doing just that and years later I spoke to Jim about it and through the wonders of Facebook sent him a copy. He took it all in good grace and admitted that he may have got his quote wrong.

With 3 minutes to go it looked like the Broch were going to have a great win but a second goal from McMaster and a last-minute winner from Alex McLeish spoilt the party.

I got a lift back to Aberdeen on their team bus that day which felt good as their Management Team spoke to me and said that I had played well and given them problems and wished me all the best at Montrose.

The Fraserburgh boys told me that the club had bought some new goal nets and a small tractor for the park with the money they got from my transfer to Montrose. They had great delight in telling me that the tractor was more agile than me!!

I loved my time at Fraserburgh and love going back to sample their hospitality. I was voted Supporters' Player of the Year that season and it is one of my most prized football awards. It is the only Player of the Year trophy that I got in my career and that is maybe why.

That, plus there was a song in the charts by Elvis Costello that year called "Oliver's Army". The Broch fans started to sing it at the games. That was special.

Above: Taking on Aberdeen's Neil Cooper in Bertie Bowie's testimonial match

Below: Scoring against Jim Leighton to put Fraserburgh 2-1 up v Aberdeen

Above/Right:
Receiving my Supporters' Player of the Year award at our end of season do

Chapter 8

Montrose (Pt. 1)

Bobby Livingstone, the Montrose manager, worked about 200 yards from me in Aberdeen and in the run up to the beginning of the season I met him a few times.

My Fraserburgh colleague, Willie Donald, worked alongside Bobby and was a good personal friend of his. It was Willie that tipped Bobby off that I might be a useful acquisition for Montrose.

Bobby is a legend at Montrose FC and was a very skilful forward who played in some of their biggest ever wins in the 70's. He had become manager the previous season while still a player, but he decided to stop playing and concentrate on being a manager. He would still join in at the shooting drills and games at training but was conspicuous by his absence at the running.

I remember my first night meeting the players for pre-season training. Bobby arranged for me to be picked up by the young centre half John Sheran at the top of Holburn Street.

I had to look out for John in his Austin 1100 and he picked me up dead on time and took me up to the Highlander Hotel at Altens where the rest of the squad met. John had a great career at Montrose FC and later became the Manager of the Club. He is still involved in football and is presently the Director of Football at Cove Rangers FC. As well as being a very successful football Manager with Cove Rangers he is also a very successful businessman in Aberdeen. Back then he was just a big country loon.

When we got to the pick-up place there was a mini-bus there and everyone got in and there were two new additions myself and Mike Milne. I had actually met Mike when training with Rosslyn Sports and it was good to see at least one face I knew.

The times in the minibus are legendary. It was an extension to the dressing room where the banter was full on and you had to be on your guard for being caught out by someone. The driver of the bus at that time was Ronnie Cross or Crosser. Ronnie was responsible for scouting the majority of the lads on the bus for Montrose and all the guys looked up to him.

Some of the guys I met for the first time that night were Stuart Beedie, Keith Joss, Alec Wright, Kenny Taylor, Colin Walker, Alex Walker, Dennis D'arcy. Ian Hair and last but not least the guy who kept us all amused on the bus Bob Cormack. Bob was a born comedian and would tell us stories about his life living in the same house as his mother-in-law, or Hinging Mince as he affectionately called her.

When Montrose were doing their pre-season training, they used to go out to "The Farm" a few miles outside Montrose. I had been trying to get myself fit and was actually feeling really fit as on top of hard training I had not been drinking for several weeks. I had been doing long hard runs and on one of these runs I caught the attention of the police.

I was not in training gear and was running in my ordinary clothes as I was making my way home from my girlfriends flat around midnight. I was running down Union Street through the week around midnight and had just passed the Music Hall when I saw a police car coming up Union Street. At this point I was going quite fast and I would gradually build up speed as I got closer to King Street and the last couple of hundred yards on King

Street was nearly flat out. The speed I was running attracted their attention and they turned and caught up with me as I turned on to King Street. I had to stop and was trying to tell them between breaths that I wasn't running away from anyone or anything but that I was just trying to get fit. I must have looked guilty.

At the Farm we would have to do some long runs with a medicine ball and I remember not being troubled too much by it and as Bobby was taking the training there would always be games and shooting that he could join in on. We had a few weeks of hard training and then we went on our Highland Tour. This was a week based in Forres and we had some games lined up against Highland League teams. Our first game was against Huntly on our way up to Forres on the Saturday.

I had been on the receiving end of some "robust" challenges from Huntly defenders the previous season when with Fraserburgh and knew that the same guys would be gunning for me again. We won the game 4-0 and I managed to score all 4 of our goals.

A great start to my playing time at Montrose and when we got to Forres I decided to have a few beers to celebrate. After not drinking for several weeks, it felt good to have a cold beer or two. Maybe it was a reaction to not having had any for a while but I got drunk very easily that night and myself and Kenny Taylor ended up at a dance out in the country a bit from Forres and we never got back in time for the curfew. We had a short training session on the Sunday because of the game on the Saturday and I managed to get through it.

We also played Forres when we were there and I think it was 2-2. It was great having a week to get to know the rest of the players and we had some laughs in the hotel and on the golf course as well as on the training grounds.

On the night before we left the hotel I had once again missed the curfew time and thought that I would climb up the drainpipe that went close to Alec Wright's bedroom window. As I got up there, I had to lean over and knock on the window with one hand while holding on with the other. I felt my hand slipping just as Alec opened the window so I let go off the drainpipe and grabbed the ledge just as Alec dropped the sash window on to my hands. He eventually managed to open the window and I was able to clamber in. There was a 10ft drop on to a glass roof below me so I was not too pleased at Wrighty dropping the window on my hands.

We had our last pre-season match on the Saturday before the season started and it was against Wigan Athletic at Links Park. The Manager of Wigan was Ian McNeill who had been the Manager at Ross County when I went there for training on Sunday mornings. It was nice to meet him again and also George Urquhart who had been at County back then. Prior to going to Dundee United I had played a couple of games for Ross County as a trialist and Ian had asked me to sign for them but I was advised not to. We played out a hard game which ended up 0-0 and I know I had a good game against a big strong Centre Half Neil Davids. A few times on the pitch we were dishing it out to one another and this was to be a source of fun in the future.

Our first game that season was away to Cowdenbeath and I was looking forward to making my league debut for Montrose. When we got to Cowdenbeath I was welcomed by big Dave Cooper my goalkeeping friend and Billy Steele a former flat mate from my time at Dundee United.

Dave and Billy had been released from United and had signed for Cowdenbeath. We had a chat before the game and were winding each other up about who was going to win. When the game started, I got a chance within the first minute and Dave made up my mind for me on what I should do, as he left his line and the ball dropped nicely for me to head it over him. I can still hear him say "Oh no..." as he was stranded in no man's land.

It turned out to be the first goal scored in the Scottish League that season. We were winning 2-1 with a couple of minutes to go to half time when we were awarded a penalty. Having scored from the spot against Huntly I confidently grabbed the ball. Dave Cooper came up to me and said "Just remember Jim I know where you put them" I usually hit them hard and low to the goalies right but this time decided to change and Dave saved it. It was a turning point as Billy scored just after half time and they added another couple to run out 4-2 winners. It was a disappointing start to our league campaign. When I think back, we had a lot of good young players, but we were inconsistent. As well as the aforementioned players we also had our South contingent of Gary Murray, Dougie Robb, Jim Moffat and Charlie Downie.

We had a great bunch of lads from Aberdeen playing for Montrose and we socialised a lot together. We would all go back to the Dutch Mill on Queens Road after the home games and the married or settled guys would have a couple and then be picked up or get a taxi home. The rest of us were ready to head in to town to sample the joys of the Grill, Bridge Bar and the The Hayloft before making our way in to Fusion (or Confusion as Alec Wright used to call it).

From there everyone was on their own and our next time of meeting anyone was 12.30pm at the Dutch Mill on the Sunday. The Sunday sessions were either quiet affairs or ended up in all day sessions. There did not seem to be an in between. Garden Parties or picnics out by the river Dee before getting ready for work on Monday. They were great times as we were all growing up together.

Some fantastic bonds made and life time friendships starting. The Montrose guys have a Former Player Reunion usually at a home game in late January early February each season and they are very well attended. It is great to meet all the old team mates and you just pick up where you left off from. You also get to meet players who have represented the club before and after your time and new friendships have been made. Last year there was an added dimension for me as in Jimmy Fotheringham I had a fellow Lilywhite to engage with.

Season 1979-80 was also Montrose FC's Centenary Year and the club had arranged a friendly with Bristol Rovers on the 26th September. The Player Manager of Rovers was Terry Cooper of Leeds United fame and he was a tremendous player and you could see it in his display that night. Montrose however put on a terrific display and we won the game 4-1. I wish someone had thought about filming the match that night as I scored the first goal that night and it was one of my best ever goals. The fact that it came from an accurate pass from Ian Hair also makes it noteworthy!! We were all given commemorative jugs of Whisky that night and I shared the contents with my grandfather and my father. I still have the empty jug in my sitting room cabinet at home as it is a tremendous memory of a great night and a great club.

Looking back now I think my own performance that season mirrored the clubs in that I was very inconsistent and would have a couple of good games get a few goals then go off the boil and struggle a bit.

We were sitting about 4th in the league and our game against the League leaders Meadowbank Thistle was due to take place on New Year's Day at Montrose.

Several of the Aberdeen lads met for a drink early on New Year's Eve in the Zebra Lounge in Aberdeen with the intention of going home after one or two. However, the heavens opened and about 1 foot of snow fell in Aberdeen that night and we all thought the game would be off.

The next morning, I called the Manager from a phone box on Union Street to hopefully hear him say that the game is off only to hear that there was

Montrose F.C. 1979-80

Back Row L to R: Derek Daun, Brian D'Arcy, Ian Hair, Gary Murray, Jim Moffat, Kenny Taylor, Charlie Downie, Alex Wright & Stuart Beedie

Front Row L to R: Bobby Livingstone (manager), Colin Walker, Bob Cormack, James Oliver, Alan Forrest, Harry Johnston, Mike Milne & Dougie Robb

Montrose celebrate in fine style

MONTROSE 4, BRISTOL ROVERS 1

MONTROSE celebrated their centenary in fine style, with a convincing victory over Second Division Bristol Rovers at Links Park.

Crowd-puller in the English side was 35-year-old Terry Cooper, the 20 times capped ex-Leeds full back. Operating deep on the left, he delighted the 800 fans with his display of close skills and distribution.

Montrose took the lead in the 17th minute. OLIVER took a Hair through ball in his stride to blast a 20-yearder past Thomas. Their lead lasted exactly five minutes, former Eire international DENNEHY netting from a Penny pass.

The homesters went ahead again in the 28th minute, when ENGLAND turned a Robb cross into his own net.

Hesitancy by the same defender cost Bristol a third goal four minutes later. He carelessly lost the ball to Robb, and his pass was swept home by MURRAY.

Fourteen minutes after the break MURRAY took the Montrose tally to four, when he wheeled on a Hair throw in to beat Thomas low at the near post with a 12-yard shot.

MONTROSE — Moffat (Charles); Hair, B. D'Arcy, Downie, Shirran (Taylor), Johnston, Milne (Beedie), Dunn, Murray (Wright), Oliver, Robb (A. Walker).

BRISTOL ROVERS — Thomas; Palmer, Baxter, England (Griffiths), Harding, Aitken, Petts (Clark), Mabbutt, Dennehy, Penny (Brown), Cooper.

Referee — A. C. Harris, Dundee.

Above
Match report from Bristol Rovers friendly

Below
Montrose FC centenary jug

no snow in Montrose and that the game was on.

We were due to go down early and have a training session followed by a pre-match meal in the Links Hotel. Bobby would pick me up on King Street on his way in to town from the Bridge of Don but I had to ask him to pick me up on Union Street as I had not got home.

When he picked me up, I got in the car and wished him a Happy New Year and he reciprocated and then asked, "Have you been out?"

I couldn't deny it and said that I thought the game would be off with all the snow that had fallen.

When we got up to the Highlander Hotel it was obvious that I had not been the only one who had been out. One lad was being sick behind his car and the others were not much better.

We went down to Montrose in a silent minibus as everyone was dreading first of all a training session and then a game against the League Leaders. When we got to Links Park there was a ray of light for us as the pitch was frozen solid but we went out and did our warm up session and it was a comedy of errors with the state of the pitch and the state of the players not conducive to a highly technical run out.

I had never seen the Manager so angry. He threatened us all that none of us would ever play football again if we let him down that day. One of Bobby's sayings was that if you were not doing well, he would "Haul you aff" and we had visions of this being the case. We were told that Meadowbank had come up the night before and had stayed in the Links Hotel, which was more bad news as they were well rested.

Our last hope was that the referee would deem the pitch unplayable but that hope was dashed when he gave the thumbs up for the game to go ahead. This was the only game that was on in the whole of the UK that day as all other games in Scotland had been called off and the English games were to be played the following day.

Bobby gave us one more warning before we went out and on a beautiful but cold day in Montrose we kicked off. About 2 minutes in to the game we got a free kick on the right about half way in to Meadowbank's half. Kenny Taylor floated a lovely ball in to the box and I met it perfectly with a header to put us 1-0 up! I celebrated by getting my arms round that other lads while they helped me back to the half way line.

After 16 minutes we got a second when the coolest guy I ever played football with, Harry Johnston, slotted in our second. We were playing them off the park and it was easily one of our best performances of the season so far. When we got in at half time Bobby didn't know what to say I think he had had visions of ripping us apart for letting him and the club down. I think he actually may have been a bit stunned by how we performed, I think we all were.

In to the second half and it was only 2 minutes old when I latched on to a pass and steered it past the outrushing goalie to put us 3-0 up. At this stage we were pushing the ball about confidently and playing lots of one-twos and we had obviously adapted to the underfoot conditions better than our opponents.

However, with about half an hour to go they got a goal back and this triggered a collapse from us. With 20 minutes to go they got a second and then with 10 minutes to go they got a third to make it 3-3.

We managed to hang on and got a 3-3 draw. When we got in to the dressing room Bobby had a go at us for being 3-0 up at home and not getting the win but secretly if anyone had offered us a 3-3 draw with the league leaders at 3.00pm we would have bitten their hands off. Bobby later that day said what the hell am I going to do with you to which I replied "How about buying me a pint?"

The first goal I got that day was the first goal scored in the 1980's in any professional football played in the whole of the UK. Having also scored the first goal of the Scottish League season at Cowdenbeath it gave me a strange double for that season.

The following week our game away to Brechin was postponed due to a frozen pitch and we got the chance to play against First Division St Johnstone. I had scored early on with a header to put us 1-0 up then I ran through and while going round the keeper we both landed on the ground and I flicked it in to the net to put us 2-0 up. While lying on the ground with the goalkeeper I realised it was friend of mine from the Highlands. It was Hamish Morrison whom I had first met in school football and then at Brora Rangers. We were to become team mates in later years but right at that moment on the pitch it was quite surreal. I said "Hamish how are you getting on?" he replied "Not so good right now" and I shook his hand and said I would see him after the game.

 People must have been wondering what the hell was going on. I always reminded him about these goals and how it should have been a hat trick as I smashed one off the bar as well.

There was a young lad playing in midfield for St Johnstone who scored an absolute screamer for them. His surname was McCoist and he pulled the score back to 2-1 but Bob Cormack got a third for us and we ran out 3-1 winners.

I wonder whatever happened to that lad McCoist? I met him in London long after he had finished playing and introduced myself to him and reminded him that I only played against him once but outscored him on the day!

In the League Cup that year we were close to pulling off a shock win when we played Hibs in the 2nd Round. The first leg was at Easter Road and we put up a great performance to hold them to a narrow 2-1 defeat. On the Saturday we played them at Links Park and after 90 minutes it was 1-0 to us and we went in to extra time and they unfortunately got the goal which

The Three Amigos in Saturday night mode. Alec Wright, Stuart Beedie and a curly headed me.

seen them go through. It was however a great experience to beat a Premier League team over the 90 minutes.

The rest of our season after January was very inconsistent and we had great wins and terrible defeats. Bobby spoke to me near the end of the season and said that he was unsure if he wanted to take up the second year of my contract or not. He said if he could have the focussed Jimmy O then it would be Yes but if he was to get more of the same then probably No. He said that he wanted time to think about it and that he would get back to me. I understood where he was coming from because when I cut out the drink and the shenanigans and got on with the job in hand, I knew I was capable of being a match winner.

I was at an Elkie Brooks concert in Aberdeen one night and I got a tap on the shoulder from someone and looked round to see Bobby. He said that

Wigan Athletic had been in touch with Montrose and would like to speak to me about a possible move to them. Bobby asked what I thought of this and I said that I would be happy to speak to them. This probably triggered the taking up of my second year of the contract! The club had already sold Gary Murray that summer to Hibs for a fee of around £70K and now a second striker was due to go as well.

I had a feeling inside me that I still wanted to give full time football a real go and that I had not fulfilled my potential when at Dundee United. I felt that Wigan would be a good move for me as there was someone there who believed I could do it as he had tried several times to sign me. I had a dilemma on my hands. I wanted to try and give full time football another chance and if I could be that focussed guy, I was sure that I could do it. I was however remembering how lost I felt when I was freed by United and I had no job or trade to fall back on.

Time to go and visit Mr McNeill in Wigan.

Chapter 9

Wigan Athletic

Wigan had been admitted in to the English 4th Division in 1979-80 and were going full time in an effort to climb up through the leagues. I had a dilemma on my hands. I was close to starting the 4th year of my apprenticeship as a Structural Engineering Technician and finishing this was important to me.

I travelled down to Wigan one Friday morning by train from Aberdeen. I was met at the Railway Station by Ian McNeill and he took me to Springfield Park where I met several of the backroom staff.

It looked a very well-run club, and the people were very friendly. I spoke to Mr McNeill and said that I would love to try full time football again but that I also wanted to finish my apprenticeship. I said that I could go back to Aberdeen and do another year there and play for Montrose and hopefully he would wait another year for me. He said what if we can get you a job down here where you can finish your apprenticeship? I said if they could do that, I would be very interested. He said that he would make some calls and would speak to me the next day.

He took me to the Hotel they had booked for me and he said that some friends would be round to meet me later. Later that night George Urquhart and Graham Willox called at the hotel to take me out on the town at

Wigan.

George had been a player at Ross County under Mr McNeil and Graham had been a very promising young lad at Ross County however he was not signed by Wigan.

I remember the first place they took me to was called The Bees Knees. It was Friday night, and the place was rocking we went in. Holding court was the big centre half Neil Davids, who I nearly came to blows with in the pre-season friendly against Wigan. Unfortunately, Neil died in 2011 but he was some character. He said, "Thank f*** you are joining us and not someone else."

I said that I had not made up my mind yet as the club were trying to sort something out for me.

Neil was a charmer with the women and I remember that night he was saying to all the girls that they needed to help out Wigan Athletic FC by making sure that I had such a good night in Wigan that I would want to come back. We certainly had a good night but I was aware that I had an early start to meet Mr McNeill and that I had to catch a train back to Aberdeen.

When I got to the ground Mr McNeill told me that he had spoken to the company that were building the new stand at Springfield Park and that they were going to give me a job in their drawing office where I could complete my apprenticeship. The owner of the company appeared, at least I think it was him, and said that this was what would happen. I thought that this would be a great compromise and agreed that if something could be sorted out between the clubs then I would be happy to join them. We spoke about a wage and as it was 4 times what I was currently on that also helped to make up my mind. I do however think it was the crowd in the Bees Knees that made up my mind!!

I went back to Aberdeen and told Bobby that I wanted to give it a go and the clubs agreed a fee.

All that was left was for me to do was tell my boss Tom White, who had given me the opportunity to start my apprenticeship, that I was going to leave. I found it really hard to do this as he had given me an opportunity to get my life back on the rails when I needed someone to help me and I will always be indebted to him. He was delighted for me at getting another chance to play full time football as he remembered the guy who had climbed the stairs so many times with the damaged knees and had taken an interest in my journey up through the various levels in part time football.

As the company also helped me with the flat by taking it on a company let this meant that the guys in the flat had to take on the lease of the flat as the company were terminating the lease. I took a lot of my belongings back up to the Highlands and dumped them in my mother and fathers' garage until I could decide what I wanted to take with me to Wigan. I said my farewells to my friends in Aberdeen and after a couple of weeks at home I made my way to Wigan.

Once again, I was walking into a new dressing room and having to get used to meeting new faces and new teammates. It helped that I knew the manager and George Urquhart. I had also met one of the other players in Aberdeen when he was signed by Aberdeen. I had met Noel Ward a couple of times while out with one of my flat mates George Campbell who played at Aberdeen as well. Noel was recovering from a very bad leg break when I arrived at Wigan and indeed, he never did recover from it. Through the wonders of Facebook, I have got back in touch with Noel, and he is still living in Wigan where he has legendary status for being part of the team that gained league status.

I was moved in to a flat on Ormskirk Road and was told that I may have to share with someone. There were two flats next door to each other which the club had and first of all Lawrence Tierney ex Hearts and Hibs moved in to the other one. Lawrence however enjoyed his home comforts and moved to be a lodger in a house.

We had just finished a hard week's training and I had been performing well. I went out on the Sunday night for a couple of beers and ran back to the flat. When I got there my new flat mate was there. It was Bobby Hutchinson ex Hibs, Dundee and Montrose. I had met Bobby a few times over the previous years. First of all, when I was at Dundee United, he was across the road at Dundee. Then when I was at Fraserburgh, Bobby was part of the Hibs team that played in the Access 5-a-Sides. I knew his pal Mitch Bavidge and I got to know him a little then. What I knew of him was that he loved a pint and he was to be my new flat mate! The worst thing about Bobby was that he could drink pints all night and still be first at the running the next day at training, whereas I couldn't! He was a great lad but looking back he was my worst nightmare as a flat mate.

I had a good start at Wigan scoring in my first game against Runcorn in a pre-season friendly and I was going quite well at Training in spite of going for a few beers with Bobby most nights. We met a Wigan supporter called Neil who recognised us in a pub and he lived just up the road from us in Ormskirk. He had a blue scooter and he used to work in the Heinz factory in Wigan. He told us that he could get us tins of Heinz food for next to nothing if we could give him tickets for the games. It seemed like a good deal for us in the flat until Neil turned up with his first bag full of tins. There were no labels on the tins so you did not know what would be inside them. The only ones that we definitely knew were the Heinz Steamed Puddings that were in a large flat tin. We would have to open several tins before we found what we were needing.

I went to speak to the Manager when I got there about my job with the company that were doing the new stand. He said to me that we would get on to it when we finished the pre-season training. As we were approaching

Wigan Athletic F.C. 1980-81

Back Row L to R: Tony Quinn, Mick Quinn, George McAllister, Lawrence Tierney, Jeff Wright, Paul Henry, David Tait

Middle Row L to R: Ian Gillibrand (trainer), George Urquhart, James Oliver, Neil Davids, John Brown, Bob Ward, Colin Methven, Peter Houghton, Frank Corrigan & Kenny Banks (trainer)

Front Row L to R: Maurice Whittle, Mark Wignall, John Curtis, Tommy Gore, Ian McNeill (manager), Dave McMullan, Bobby Hutchinson, David Glenn & David Fretwell

A day out at Blackpool with team mates Lawrence Tierney & Bobby Hutchinson

the end of the pre-season training, I again asked and was shocked to be told that the Club were in a dispute with the company over the work that was getting done at the stadium. This meant that I could not go and work with them and I could not finish my apprenticeship. This was a dark moment for me which wasn't helped when I picked up an injury in a game at Southport which meant that I was on the treatment table for the start of the season.

The main striker from the previous season was Peter Houghton and he was playing well as was Bobby Hutchinson and one of our young lads Micky Quinn was showing a bit of promise. Micky's cousin Tony was also there as a forward and I found myself way down the pecking order for a place in the first team squad. I played most games for the reserves but if any of the guys ahead of you were needing games then you would sometimes not even get a game there. Fred Eyre who ran the second team asked me if I fancied playing centre half one night. I always prided myself in that I thought that I could give a good account of myself in any position. Looking back at it maybe I should have given the centre back position a go as I got good reviews for my performances. I look at how well other centre forwards have done by going back in to defence. Paul Hegarty and Colin Hendry are two that spring to mind. I'm not saying I could have got to their standard but it may have prolonged my full-time career.

I kept plugging away in the reserves and at training and eventually I got a chance to get back in to the team away to Darlington. The team did not play well that day and we lost 3-1 and I feel as though I was made one of the scapegoats that day. I remember that I was on my own in front of goal and a cut back from a team mate would have left me to roll it in to the net. This would have given us the lead but this person chose to shoot from an acute angle and the goalkeeper saved it. I was taken off in the second half and faded back in to the reserves.

My hopes of getting back in to the reckoning for the first team faded even further as the club signed Billy Urquhart from Glasgow Rangers. Billy was an out and out striker and this put me even further out of the picture. Billy had come down with his fiancée Patricia to speak to Wigan and they took in a game. We all went out at night and had a few beers and I think Patricia pulled the wedding forward 6 months after seeing what nights out were like in Wigan!

I spoke to the manager again about how pissed off I was about my apprenticeship falling by the wayside and I asked if I could get some time off to go and see if I could get my old job back in Aberdeen. I was given permission to go back to Scotland to try and get myself a job and if possible, a team. The manager said that as the club had let me down over the job, they would allow me to go on a free transfer.

It was the second week in December and my friend Steve Cook from

PLAYER

James David Oliver
(Striker)
Birthplace: **Fearn, Ross, Scotland**
Place of Residence: **Pemberton, Wigan**
Date of Birth: **13th January, 1958**
Height: **6'0"**
Weight: **13st. 3lbs.**
Previous Professional Clubs: **Brora Rangers, Dundee United, Ross County, Fraserburgh & Montrose.**
Advice to Youngsters: **Work hard at your ball control, and try to make every attempt at goal count.**

"Big Jim" has had few opportunities to show his true worth since coming down from North of the Border. However, Fred Eyre's recent experiment with this strong player in a defensive role has been an interesting development.

Photo by courtesy of The Wigan Reporter

PORTRAIT

Aberdeen came down to see me in Wigan and we had a great Fancy Dress night out in the Turnkey Cellars where I was dressed up as a Convict, Steve as a Clown and Bobby Hutch as a Gollywog. Bobby had misread the directions on the theatrical make up that he used. Instead of putting some on and spreading it around his face he layered it on thick and you could see anyone that he had come in to contact with as they were all black from his close attention. Billy Urquhart was there as Bill Haley and we were all Rocking around the Clock that night.

I went back to Aberdeen with Steve and I went in and spoke to my old boss but they did not have a position as they had filled the role with someone else. They did however say to me that I had overpaid on the rent in the flat by just over £1000 and they gave this money to me a week before Christmas. Steve had his birthday on the 18th of December, and we had a party in his house with his teammates from Turriff United. The whole of the Christmas Holidays turned in to a drink fest.

I had talks with Peterhead FC about joining them but I needed that job to finish off my apprenticeship and they could not help. I was also not sure how my Fraserburgh friends would have viewed me signing for their arch rivals.

Steve and I headed up to the Highlands for a few days and while we were there, we were involved in a car accident and ended upside down in a deep ditch filled with icy water. I was on the bottom under the water as people were getting out of the car and I was last to get out. It was early in the morning and it was absolutely freezing and we were soaking. I ended up getting a horrendous cold which turned in to more of a flu and I was in bed for about a week.

During this time the club had been trying to get in touch with me as they had a mounting injury list and they said they needed me back. I was in no fit state to travel far less play. I eventually got back to Wigan in early

January to be told that the club were suspending me without pay for two weeks. They said that I was absent without permission which was not the case as I was given permission to go to Scotland to try and secure a job and a team if possible.

I was put in touch with the Professional Footballers Union and after hearing my side of the argument they agreed to fight my case.

I had to attend a tribunal in London with Mr McNeill and we were both taken in and were asked to relate our version of the events. When the panel heard of the breaking of the promise of a job to finish my apprenticeship that was the deciding factor. Mr McNeill admitted that the club had let me down and the suspension was lifted.

We had to travel back together on the train and I took the opportunity to apologise to Mr McNeill for some of my behaviour and I told him that all I wanted to do was play football for him. There was a reserve match that night and I asked him if I could play in it and he said I could. We actually had a very good conversation all the way back to Wigan and I felt more at ease for the first time in months. When we got back to the club it was not long before kick-off. I walked in to the dressing room and all the guys looked at me wondering how I had got on. I just gave a thumbs up. I played that night we won and I scored.

I am not sure if that episode had anything to do with Mr McNeill losing his job, I certainly hope it didn't and I met him in Nairn many years later and apologised to him in case it had something to do with it. He told me that it wasn't that and it was a mixture of many things that led to him being removed from his role.

We were all told that Mr McNeill was being replaced and that our new Manager would be revealed soon. While I knew Mr McNeill and trusted him that he would give me another chance I thought with the new manager I will have a clean slate and hopefully I could impress him.

We were all asked to come up in to the Boardroom a few days later and we were introduced to our new Manager. It was Larry Lloyd who had played for Nottingham Forest and Liverpool. He was a big man maybe 6' 3" or 6' 4" and he was a bully. He spoke to us all and said that he was the boss and what he said went. One of the players Frank Corrigan from Liverpool then said "We will just set Big Jim on you". Lloyd said "who the f*** is Big Jim?" They all looked towards me and I am thinking Thanks Frank. The new man hasn't even started and I am his target already.

Lloyd then arranges a game on Springfield Park for the First Team against the Second Team and he is Centre Half for the First Team and I am Centre Forward for the Second Team. Not long in to the game the ball comes up to my feet and I go to go one way but use the outside of my foot to go the other way and he cleans me out with a tackle. It is an obvious foul and everyone stops and he shouts "Play on". I am raging about this but don't say anything and when I am back for a corner against us, I say to our goalie. "Next time you get the ball hang one up in the air between me and him". The goalkeeper does this and I give him plenty of room to come through to head it but as he does, I elbow him in the face and as everyone stops, I shout, "Play on".

He takes me in to his office and he is raging and said don't you ever do anything like that again or your feet won't touch the ground going out of here. I replied to him that he started it and if someone has a go at me on the park I will fight back. It got me back in to the first team squad but it was only temporary as he said he did not like "Sweaty Socks". That was a bit of a cheek coming from a man who played with the likes of John Robertson, Archie Gemmill, Kenny Burns and John McGovern at Nottingham Forest. The man was a bully and I couldn't stand him.

I was in contact with some clubs back in Scotland and told them all that I needed a job where I could finish off my apprenticeship. I spoke with

Inverness Caledonian, Elgin City and Peterhead but nothing materialised on the job front. I stayed at Wigan and trained and played in the reserves but I was desperate to get away so I agreed a compensation package with them and went back to Aberdeen.

I came to Wigan determined to give full time football a real go but after getting injured, the disappointment of being let down over the job and my own subsequent indiscipline meant that there was no way back after that.

I liked the people of Wigan and had some fantastic times and even got to play in the same 5-a-Side team as Bobby Charlton (now Sir Bobby). Bobby was a director at the club and he would join in training some days. He would have been in his mid 40's at the time but you could see he was a magnificent footballer and such a sweet striker of the ball. I recall him describing one of my shots at goal against York City as one of the hardest shots he had ever seen!! I took that as a massive compliment but thought maybe he was not counting his own shots in that statement.

I moved back to Aberdeen, and some help in finding a new job and a club to play for came from an old friend.

Chapter 10

Montrose (Pt. 2)

When I moved back to Aberdeen, I had no job and with a small compensation payment from Wigan I set about getting back into a job where I could finish my apprenticeship.

Steve Cook arranged it with his parents for me to stay in his house in Caledonian Place until I found somewhere to live in Aberdeen. Mrs Cook was a very good cook and I was not used to eating so much after looking after myself in flats for the previous 3-4 years. After about 3 weeks I moved to a bed sit which was not ideal but would have to do in the interim. If I had stayed at the Cook's, I would have been 20 stone within months.

I met with Bobby Livingstone and he told me he knew of a job that was going out at Inverurie which would allow me to finish off my apprenticeship. The company was Seaforth Engineering and the HR person was Doug McIldowie who was from Invergordon and had played for Woodacon when I was at Rosslyn.

I spoke with Doug and was asked to attend an interview out at Seaforth Engineering at Inverurie. I attended the interview and was given an offer of the job following this. As well as helping me to get this job Bobby asked me if I would consider coming back to Montrose. As I had only been away 1 season most of the guys were still there and it was easy to fit back in to the group. The fact that I had been training full time showed as I was flying during our pre-season training and games and was scoring freely.

On the last weekend before the season started, we had two games arranged against Highland League opposition. We were to play Deveronvale at Banff on the Saturday and then Huntly at Huntly on the Sunday. Bobby was going to play his entire squad over the two games.

On the Saturday at Banff, we won 2-0 and I scored both goals. Bobby was happy with how I had been performing and told me that I would probably not be used against Huntly as I had shown enough to be starting when the league games commenced the following Saturday.

During the game against Huntly, we had fallen behind and our Centre Half John Sheran took a nasty injury to his leg. I was put on and pulled us level before taking a knock at the top of my ankle and could not play on. As Bobby was taking John into Aberdeen Royal Infirmary in his car, they thought that I might as well go as well. The news was not good about John as he had a badly broken leg and then the doctor told me that I had broken my leg just above my ankle.

This was a shattering blow to all three of us. Bobby had lost his Centre Half and Centre Forward a week before the season was about to start and both John and I were likely to be out for several months. As it transpired, I got back playing in January and John did not play at all that season.

I was shattered as the injury jinx that had hit me at the beginning of the previous season had once again hit me. I also had to make my way back and fore to Inverurie to get to work. I was thankful to a colleague Alan Glennie from Stonehaven who came round by Aberdeen to pick me up to take me to Inverurie on a daily basis as I was unable to drive.

During the time I had the plaster on I actually broke the cast 3 times and had to go back to the hospital to get the cast reset. One of the times I broke it was as I was attempting to get in to Fusion Night Club in Aberdeen. I was on crutches and the doormen told me that I could not get in with the crutches. I handed them the crutches and said that I did not need them and promptly fell out the door and down the steps cracking the cast. They did not let me in.

One Sunday I was sitting in the Inn at the Park with a few of the lads and Alex Ferguson, who was Manager at Aberdeen at the time, came over to our table and asked me by name how my leg was. I did not even think he would know me. He wished me all the best and hoped that I would get back playing again soon as they had been watching me!!

I don't know when their interest in me had begun but I think it may have been when I played in Bertie Bowies Testimonial Match and had a good display against a strong Aberdeen team. Many years later I was to hear a story about why Aberdeen or Fergie had not signed me. I would love to find out if it is true but only Fergie would know and I don't know him well enough to ask.

I was in plaster for about 8 weeks and then I had to go to ARI to get it removed. I got it removed one Monday and we were training at Montrose that night. My legs are quite big and when the cast came off, I thought someone had transplanted one of Ghandi's legs on to me as the muscle had wasted away and I had this thin stick like appendage in its place.

When we got down to Links Park I wanted to get out and get running but did not realise how weak it was and I fell in a heap right away. I was given exercises to build up the muscle and I was sent down to the seaside at Montrose to wiggle my ankle in the wet sand at the water's edge. Montrose beach on a Monday night in October is not the warmest place to be.

Gradually my leg strengthened and I was able to join in the bulk of the training but needed some game time to get back in shape. I remember playing against a Dundee United reserve team and coming up against Walter Smith. I was trying really hard and Walter told me to take it easier as it was important not to overdo it so soon. I managed to score in that game which was a confidence booster. I eventually got back in to the 1st team in early January as I was one of the subs in our home game v our near neighbours Brechin City.

Brechin were going well under the stewardship of Archie Knox whom I knew from my days at Tannadice. We were getting beaten 2-0 at half time and not long after half time Bobby put me on. Not long after coming on I nodded the ball down to Mike Turnbull in the six-yard box and he pulled one back. With time running out I played the ball out to the wing and as the winger got into the box and cut it back to me I lashed it in to the net for an equaliser. Scoring that goal after being out for so long was one of the best feelings ever.

Around the end of February Bobby Livingstone parted company with the club and I think Denis D'arcy took over temporarily while the club looked for another manager. I have spoken to Bobby many times since then and he maintains that the pre-season injuries to John Sheran and myself were devastating blows for him and the team never got going properly after that. I was in and out of the team at this time as I lacked fitness from being out for so long through injury.

The new Manager was announced with a few weeks to go to the end of the season and it was Steve Murray who had played for Celtic and Aberdeen. Steve was a fitness fanatic and the first thing he said to me was that he was not playing me until I got down to 13st 4lbs, which he reckoned was my ideal weight for my height and build.

He told me that he would like me to go without food and booze for a week to get to my fighting weight. Drinking only water and tea from that Monday nights training session for the rest of the week I was doing well until I had a few beers on Sunday afternoon which turned in to a Sunday session and as I was walking up the road on Sunday night, I got the smell

A bad start to the season for John Sheran and myself

of fish & chips. A fish supper and a single red pudding later and the "No Food and Booze for a week plan" was out the window.

At training on the Monday night, we had our weigh-in and I was standing beside the Physio's table and stepped on to the scales. The dial was hovering at around 13st 4lbs and Steve Murray said "You have done it!!" then he seen my finger almost bent double on the Physio's table pushing me up the way. He told me to get my finger off the table and my weight shot up to the 13st 10lbs that I was the previous Monday night. As I was struggling to get near the 13st 4lbs (a weight I have never again achieved so far) I was only used sparingly as a sub for the rest of that season.

At the start of the following season, we had a few new signings from the Dundee and Central Belt area to complement the existing Dundee and Aberdeen based squad. As we started our pre-season training at the beach in Montrose myself and Kenny Taylor were at the front to try and set the pace. Next thing the Manager shot past us and asked us to keep up with him. This was not possible for us on the soft sand and we were getting overtaken by the lighter members of the squad. Eventually the two of us were at the back where Assistant Manager Ally Donaldson, who played in goals for Dundee for many years, was there to keep the squad moving.

Totally exhausted from running in the soft sand I stopped running and Ally encouraged me to get going again and said that I was fined £1 for stopping. I started running again but about another 100 yards along the sand I stopped again and was told that I was getting fined another £1. I was then told to start running again and I replied "If I am getting fined £1 every time I stop, I am stopping for 20 minutes. Ally then told me that I was getting fined £20 for my remarks. I found pre-season very hard and very boring. If I had wanted to be a runner, I would have joined an Athletics Club. I realise that you have to be fit to play but I find that if you do your exercises with a ball, you don't realise how much running you are doing, and the fitness comes naturally. When I went in to coaching all my coaching was done with a ball and the teams I had were usually fit.

When the season started, I was out of the starting 11 and 2 subs and with no reserve team it was difficult to get any match time. A number of the players who were in the same boat as me had fallen out with the manager and were in dispute with the club.

After not being involved for a few weeks, we made the trip down to Arbroath to face our Angus rivals. I was not expecting to play but we all had to go in to hear the team being named before leaving the dressing room to those who were involved. The players who were in dispute with the club were asked to attend the matches but were not asked in to the dressing room when the team was being announced. One of the players who was in dispute was Alex Wright and he was heading over to the Tutties Neuk pub right across the road from Gayfield. I asked him to order up a pint for me as I would be straight over once the team was named.

Steve Murray got us all in the dressing room and he said "OK Hands up those of you were out last night?". No hands went up. Okay he said let me put it another way "Hands up those of you who did not think that they would be playing today that were out last night" Again no hands went up. Okay let me put it another way "Jim were you out last night?" To which I replied "No boss I was round at my girlfriends watching TV" Oh well he said We will soon find out as you are playing midfield today. Are you up for it? I replied "Of course I am, I can play anywhere". I was asked to play left midfield and as I was two footed that was ok plus if I came inside, I was on to my stronger right foot.

I proceeded to get changed and I liked to get out early and get a few stretches and a few kicks of the ball. Gayfield was very soft that day and we were asked not to go on the playing surface to warm up.

One of the players had to get a fitness test and they were asked to go and do it on the grass beside the Tutties Neuk Bar. Just then I remembered that I had Alex Wright waiting with a pint for me in the bar. I offered to go and help with the Fitness Test and crossed the road in my full strip and boots with a warm up top covering the match day strip. I went to the window of the pub and could see Alex at the bar with the drinks in front of him and tried to get his attention. He could not hear or see me so I decided to go in and speak to him. I opened the door and walked in with my kit on and said to him that I wouldn't be able to have my pint as I was playing! The bar was full of Montrose Fans and I got a big cheer as I got on very well with the fans. Some of them were encouraging me to have a sip of beer but I managed to resist.

The game was about 2 minutes old, and I got the chance to put in a solid

The Tutties Neuk Bar in Arbroath - scene of my appearance in full Montrose FC playing kit 30 minutes before kick off v Arbroath FC. To the left is the grass area where the fitness test took place.

tackle on the edge of their 18-yard box and steamed into the tackle. I caught the ball very solidly and it flew in to the bottom corner of the net to put us 1-0 up. I thought that I had a decent game but the soft conditions caught up with me and my lack of match fitness and I came off after an hour. We lost the game 3-1 but I thought we looked more solid when I was on the park.

I flitted in and out of the team getting the occasional start but mostly sub appearances and then I got another injury which had me out for a few weeks.

The Scottish Cup draw gave us a tie away to my first Senior Club Brora Rangers. The tie was to be played in early January and I was hoping to get back fit for it. I just ran out of time to get fit but travelled to see the clubs fight out a 0-0 draw at Dudgeon Park.

The replay was the following week at Links Park and I convinced the manager in training that I was fit to play in this game. I remember Brora had 3 big defenders in Robert Allan, Robert Christie and Doug Norris and I was comfortable playing against them all as I knew them all from before. I laid on our goal for Derek Nicol to put us 1-0 up but a late McAskill goal for Brora got them a draw.

In those days the games went to a 2nd Replay on a neutral ground. The venue was Kingsmill Park Inverness the home of Inverness Thistle. When we left Montrose on Saturday, we were not aware of when or where the game would be, and we thought that we would be told at training on Monday night.

I had a day off work on the Monday and was in the flat when the doorbell went and it was Alex Wright to tell me that we were getting picked up in 15 mins by bus to go to Inverness to play Brora.

Probably not the best preparation for a game as I had been out to lunch with a young lady and she was still in the flat. We made it to the bus and there was no manager or assistant manager on the bus and the chairman told us that the manager was driving up the A9 and would meet us in Inverness.

We were sitting in the dressing room at Kingsmills with less than an hour to go when it was decided that Les Barr the most senior player should call the team. Les went with the same team from Saturday with me starting up front.

We were getting changed and one of the Directors came in with a note from the Manager who had phoned in the team from somewhere on the A9. In the revised team I was dropped to the bench.

This disappointed me but I was still glad to be in the 13. We were just about to go out for a warm up when a further message came in that I was to be taken off the subs bench and be replaced by a Centre Half. The rest of the guys could see that I was devastated not to be involved after playing so well on the Saturday. They spoke about not letting on that they got the second message but by this time I was getting dressed and was on my way to the nearest Pub. This was my first visit to the Heathmount and I had a few pints with some Brora fans who were delighted to see me in there.

Brora beat Montrose 5-2 after extra time in a match played in horrendous conditions. It was 2-2 at full time and I know that had I played that night I would have scored. Brora scored 3 in extra time and ran out worthy winners.

Steve Murray had arrived just before kick-off and I sought him out after the game and told him that I was wanting away from the club after being humiliated in front of my teammates. He said I would need to ask someone else as he had just handed in his resignation. I told him it was the best thing he had done since he came to the club.

Denis D'arcy took over temporarily and tried to persuade me to withdraw my request to be released from my contract but I was still raging and had made up my mind.

The club gave me my release and I was again looking for a club. Around this time my apprenticeship came to an end and with very little work on the books the company paid off a few of us. So now I had no club and no job. I had however completed my Structural Draughtsman apprenticeship which was a great feeling and something that I am still proud of.

Bobby Livingstone had gone up to Deveronvale in the Highland League and he contacted me to see if I fancied playing for them. I said that I would sign on for them on the proviso that if I got a better offer to go elsewhere, they would not hold on to me.

I played 2 games for the Vale and they were both Aberdeenshire Cup games v Aberdeen University and we drew the first and got beat in the replay. Before my third game an opportunity arose for me to sample football abroad and Vale freed me as agreed.

I was disappointed in how my time at Montrose ended as it is a great club and they have a superb Community presence now. The club holds an Annual Former Players Hospitality event around the end of January each year and they are brilliant get-togethers. We managed to get the 2020 one in a couple of weeks before the Covid-19 Lockdown but the 2021 one was cancelled.

Hopefully we can meet again in 2022.

Chapter 11

Ryoden (Hong Kong)

After being made redundant from my job at Seaforth Engineering, I had been searching through the Press & Journal looking for a job. On the sports pages I noticed a story about my former Wigan team mate Billy Urquhart turning down the opportunity to go and play in Hong Kong.

The article was written by Bill Mcallister whom I knew from my Highland League days. I contacted Bill and asked him if the team in Hong Kong would be interested in myself coming out to play for them as I was ready, willing and able. Bill made a call to his contact whom I believed to be ex Hibs and Meadowbank Manager Willie McFarlane and Bill got back to me to say that Willie was making contact with the people in Hong Kong.

I never heard anything for a couple of days and then I got a call from Willie asking if I could fly out to Hong Kong the following morning from Heathrow! I said yes and that I would try to get there for the flight. I then had to book a flight from Aberdeen to London. I got this organised and called Willie back to say I could make it and he told me that I had to meet a Mr Loung outside the Loon Moon Restaurant in Victoria Street London at 10.00pm that night.

My landlord, Willie Skinner from Balintore, arrived home from his two-week stint offshore at 12.00 noon and I asked him for a lift back out to the airport as I was going to Hong Kong. Willie gave me a lift out and I asked him to keep my room for me as I did not know what I was letting myself in for.

When I got to Heathrow, I asked at the Information Desk where about Victoria Street was and they asked me which one. Not a very good start when heading off half way around the world. I explained that it may be in a Chinese sector and they pointed me to what they thought was the most likely one.

When I got out of the Tube Station it was about 9.45pm and I got to the Loon Moon Restaurant a couple of minutes before 10.00pm and Mr Loung turned up a couple of minutes later. He gave me a one-way ticket to Hong Kong with British Airways, and he took me to a B&B just around the corner where I was to stay the night.

The flight was at 8.30am the next morning and I decided that I would rather be out at the airport and sleeping in a chair than having to make my way out to Heathrow after a few hours' sleep. I went back out to the Airport and found the correct Terminal and sat and watched the people in the airport. This was to become a great pastime of mine in later years as I waited in Airport Terminals for connecting flights.

Eventually the time came to board the plane and I was seated next to a Chinese couple who were all lovey dovey and giggling all the time. They were like this the whole time and it was difficult to get to sleep at all.

The flight had two stops on the way. Firstly, in Dubai and the second stop was in Bombay (or Mumbai as it is called now). At Bombay we were given the opportunity to get out into the Terminal and stretch our legs but if we left the plane, we were not allowed back on until the passengers from Bombay were boarding. This was about 2 hours and I thought as I have never been in India before it will be nice to say that I have walked on Indian soil. I can't recall what time it was when we were there, but the sun was just up and I recall getting hit by the stench of what smelt like raw sewage. I wanted to turn straight around and go back on the plane but we had to wait 2 hours. These were two long hours as I thought I was going to throw up all the time. I can still remember that taste of India.

Once we got back on the plane we flew over the likes of Thailand and Vietnam and I recall the miles and miles of sandy beaches on the Vietnamese coast. As we started our descent in to Hong Kong, I started thinking that I hope that there was someone there to meet me!! I would have been alright if Mr Loung had not turned up in London as I knew several people there but I knew no one in Hong Kong.

As the plane was banking in steeply to land at Kai Tak Airport, I seen the biggest San Miguel sign I have ever seen on the side of a building and I thought that it could be quite a good place after all.

When we landed, we were taken through customs and then picked up our luggage and we entered the Arrivals Lounge. All I could see were a sea of Chinese faces and I thought to myself "What the f*** are you doing here?" For what seemed like an age I stood there wondering how the hell I was going to get home as the realisation that it was a one-way ticket started to dawn on me.

All of a sudden, a Chinese gentleman came up to me and asked if I was Mr Oliver (although he pronounced it Oriver) and I grabbed his hand and thought, "Thank F***."

All of a sudden there was a bit of commotion in front of us as Photographers started taking photos and I looked round to see if someone famous had walked through arrivals. Then this big brash Dutch gentleman grabbed me and shook my hand and turned me towards the cameras with him. This was my first meeting with the team coach Franz Van Balkom. He was dressed in his football training kit and we were taken in to a Press Room where there were 3 chairs on a raised platform.

By this time my luggage and football bag had been taken from me by one of the team's Chinese coaches and I was invited to take the middle chair on the stage. To my right was Van Balkom and to my left was a Chinese man with a microphone. I had never been in a situation like this before as this did not happen when you played for Fraserburgh, Montrose and Wigan!!

I was very nervous as to what was going to happen next. The Chinese are a very direct nationality and they come straight to the point. The first question was "Your rivals Bulova (one of the teams in the league) have just signed Derek Parlane. Are you a better player than him?

I was formulating an answer in my head along the lines of "Derek is a very experienced player and has played for big teams such as Rangers and Manchester City and is a Scottish Internationalist..." when Van Balkom shouts "Of course he is better than him...I would not have signed him if he wasn't."

I was sitting there thinking to myself What the F** have I let myself in for!! There were a few more questions about teams that I played for and it was interesting to see the puzzled looks on their faces when I mentioned The Broch and the Gable Endies.

Van Balkom decided to take me straight to the training ground where I was kitted out with some training gear but my football boots had been taken to the flat. I therefore did a training stint in front of the reporters and photographers in my socks until a pair of size 11 boots were found. I still have a copy of the report from one of the papers and there is a photo of me looking knackered. I had had about 2 hours sleep from leaving Aberdeen so the photo was accurate. I will need to get someone to translate it for me. After my training session I was taken to the offices of Ryoden who the team was named after. They were a subsidiary of Mitsubishi that designed and manufactured Escalators and Elevators. I could not resist the old Elevator joke and said to one of the officials that business must be Up and Down to which he replied No it is very stable at the moment. I duly signed the forms and they were rushed away to be registered so that I could play on Saturday.

I was then taken by a couple of the coaches for something to eat. When the food arrived, I noticed that there was no fork and knife and all that was handed out was chopsticks. After a quick lesson from the Coaches, I was soon asking for a fork so that I could get something into my mouth instead of on to the table or the floor. Eating out in Hong Kong is an experience and one that I thoroughly enjoyed however some of their dishes were uneatable for me. I will not go in to any details but suffice to say they were not the kindest of people to animals. For the first three months I was there I thought we had a pet shop at the end of the road until I realised rather graphically one day that it was a butcher's.

I was to share a flat with Duncan McKenzie who had also signed at the same time as me. Duncan was presently in a hotel with his wife Dot and son Stephen and would move in to the flat when they went back to the UK. I had obviously heard of Duncan and his exploits of jumping over a Mini before a game at Leeds United. I did not however realise what a fantastic football player he was and what an absolute gentleman he was.

Duncan had played for the likes of Nottingham Forest, Anderlecht, Everton, Chelsea and Leeds United and has written a book about his time in football. The book finishes with his time in Hong Kong so I can say that living in a flat with me finished his career. I am delighted that he has become a lifelong friend and we have met up several times since then. Duncan is a very clever, funny and intelligent man and he does the After Dinner circuit in the UK and is a highly prized speaker commanding a sizeable fee. I have however had him help me at some of the clubs I have been with by promising him free rounds of golf at some of the Highlands' beautiful courses. When he has helped me out he has never asked for a fee

With Duncan Mackenzie & David Stewart

菱電中鋒奧利華：有牙歪鼻

撞傷皮肉司空見慣　死馬衝門戰鬥續

小小創傷　不足掛齒

戰術需要　膽正命平

多年庸碌　希望突破

高溫天氣　實在難頂

筆談

實路華對利物浦・大圭護級有計・南華留班未絕望

余國際連中三元・敗家仔可改名・禁球員被訪問・米勒措施夠霸道

What the papers had to say about my arrival

just for his travel and costs to be covered. We did give him some pocket money on one outing but took him on a pub crawl in Inverness where he ended up spending the lot!

We managed to get one day's training done before the monsoon season started and it rained for about 4 weeks. From rushing me out to play in Saturday's game we ended up being 5 weeks without a game due to the weather.

During this time, I got to know the players at the club and there was a mixture of experienced players coming to the end of their careers, some like me who had maybe lost their way a bit and the locals who were very skilful.

Each team was only allowed 4 foreigners in the team at one time. You could name 7 foreigners in your squad but if you were taking a foreigner on you had to take one off. Amongst our foreigners were Duncan, myself, David Stewart (ex Leeds United and Scotland goalkeeper), Graeme Hedley (ex Middlesbrough), Chris Lynam (ex Manchester United), Dries Visser (Dutch) and Michael Mommertz (Dutch). We also had a Liverpudlian called Bernie Poole who was classed as a local as he had been out there for so long. Graeme, Chris and a couple of the local players stayed in the same block of flats as us so they showed me how to get back and fore to training at the Happy Valley.

When I told the Aberdeen boys that we trained at the Happy Valley they said No change there then, with reference to the Aberdeen night club with the same name. Our flat was on the 17th floor of the Foo Yet Kai building in North Point on Hong Kong Island.

On Hong Kong island there is a Tram system which goes from one end of the island to the other and I was told it is a great way to discover the city and see some of the sights. I decided that I was going to have a go and get on at North Point and go right to either end and get back off at North

135

Point. I got to the Tram Stop and I was about 2nd or 3rd in the queue as the tram arrived. When the tram was about 5 yards from the stop everyone broke ranks and charged to get on the tram with the result being that I did not get on. I was ready for the next one and did not miss another one after that.

When on the tram I went upstairs and got a window seat so that I could get a good view of all that was going on in the streets. An old Chinese woman sat beside me and a little while after that she started to clear her throat and turned to spit it out the window. I sat bolt upright on the seat as this lump of green phlegm flew past me and out the window. This thing would have cracked the pavement if it landed on it.

By this time Duncan's family had gone back to the UK and he was in the flat when I got back. I told him about the old woman and he said they called it getting the devil from their throat.

Duncan had played in America for a while, and he told me about a fast-food chain that they had out there and that there was one on the corner of our block and did I want to join him for something to eat. So, we ventured down to a place called McDonalds and I had my first ever McDonald's cheeseburger and more importantly Banana Milk Shake.

The training started at 8.00am in the morning and finished at 10.00am. This was because of the heat and humidity in Hong Kong. The training sessions were good and we had a lot of exercises with the ball which ended up with getting a shot at goals. After training a few of the guys would catch a taxi to the other side of the island to Repulse Bay which was like a Mediterranean beach with bars and cafes along it. What a life! 2 hours training 5 days a week and a game on one of the other days and all this in a Holiday Resort with unbelievable night life. What was there not to enjoy? When Duncan and I joined the club, they were adrift at the bottom of the league but in the 8 league games that were played between our joining

Training at the Happy Valley with Bernie Saunders and Graham Hedley in attendance

and the end of the season we won 2, drew 5 and lost 1. The last game of the season we got beat but by this time we were safe and I scored the goal that made us safe in our second last game. I got injured in that game and was to miss the last game so I went undefeated in my time in Hong Kong. The results were enough to save the team from relegation from the Hong Kong top division. We also had friendly matches against the Hong Kong national team and The Scots Guards who were stationed at Stanley Fort. I got to know a few of the Scots Guards and had a number of crazy nights out with them that started in the Sergeants Mess at the Fort and ended up in the Wan Chai district.

There were so many crazy nights out which ended up with you going to training drunk and then sleeping it off on the beach but at that age we were able to do it. I recall one day we were sleeping off a hangover when some locals arrived with a ghetto blaster that was making the sand bounce. I got up walked over and turned it down much to their annoyance and it looked like there was going to be a bit of trouble as there were about 10 of them and 4 of us. Then about half a dozen Scots Guards who had seem what was unfolding came over and made it a more even number. The sight of the Scots Guards must have frightened them off and it was great to know that we had a peace keeping mission keeping any eye out for us.

Happy Valley Training Ground   Repulse Bay Recovery Ground

I liked a wee challenge on the drinking front and one night we were in one of our locals when Jimmy Bone came in. Jimmy was a player with Hong Kong Rangers and I had got to know him out there. Jimmy like myself enjoyed a beer and we had a few and a few more and I thought bugger it I am going to drink him under the table. So, we had a few more and then moved to another pub and another pub and I was thinking, when is he going to say we better call it a night? As we were now in a Night Club and it was around 6.30am and training started at 8.00am I thought to myself he has beaten me I had better go. I turned to him and let him know I think we better stop as training will be starting soon and he turned to me and said, "Did I not tell you that I had today off?"

I phoned Duncan in the flat and asked him to take my training gear to the Happy Valley for me as I was on the other side of Hong Kong. When I got there about 7.30am I made my way to the pitches where several of the teams trained. Some of the local players were already there and I sat down on a bench and fell asleep. I was awakened by ex-Aberdeen player Duncan Davidson saying to me, "Jim, this is not your team's pitch, your team is over there."

I replied in a drunken state "They all look the same to me!" and made my way to our pitch.

Van Balkom did not take too long to realise that I was worse for wear and had me doing quite a lot of exercises which had the desired effect for him in that I was violently sick. When I told him what had happened, he just laughed and said that he thought my dribbling was better today but not to do it again.

There were so many stories to tell about my time in Hong Kong that I could write a whole book about them on its own. There are, however, a couple that I think I should mention.

The first concerns a friendly match that we had with the Scots Guards at Stanley Fort. This was arranged through myself and Ronnie Moffat who was my best friend in the Guards. It was arranged so that the team could sample the delights of the cheap drink in the Sergeants Mess at the Fort. It was 10HK dollars (about £1) for a beer in Hong Kong but only 2HK Dollars (20p) for a pint of beer in the Mess. We won the game 12-2 and I scored a few. I was being marked by a giant of a man called Angus who was from Uist in the Outer Hebrides. I managed to keep away from any of his lunges on the pitch and then afterwards in the Mess Ronnie introduced me to him.

Angus was about 6' 20" and was about 4' wide in the chest. His arms were about the size of my legs. He also had a lisp. By this time, we had all had a few drinks and Angus said to me "I'm a better footballer than you" to which I replied, "I am a better soldier than you."

Angus replied with "I had trials for Partick Sissle", to which I said, "was that Partick Sissle or Thistle?" and he came back with "Sissle, Sissle."

The whole place erupted, and when Angus realised I was taking the piss, he grabbed me by the throat with one hand and lifted me off the ground. I was around 13st 8lbs at this time and I was dangling in the air. About half a dozen Scots Guards piled on him and got him off me. I think he would have killed me if they hadn't. A few days later he apologized to me and me to him and until I left Hong Kong, we got on great.

When we were in Hong Kong Liverpool FC came out to play a friendly against the Hong Kong National team. They had players like Dalglish, Souness, Hansen, Grobellar, Nicol, Lawrenson, Neal amongst many others. One of our players Graeme Hedley had played alongside Souness, David Hodgson and Craig Johnston at Middlesbrough. Graeme arranged for the Liverpool players to come out with us for a few beers after the game. I was looking forward to meeting with Kenny (my hero) but he and Souness and some of the other senior players went elsewhere. We did however have Hansen who was the ring leader for a number of beer games such as The Boat Race and Buzz. I will never forget Steve Nicol playing Buzz. He did not have a clue what he was doing and ended up just downing his drink when it came round to him. That was a night to remember and I was in the winning line on the Boat Race.

The scariest and maddest thing that I have ever done was done while I was in Hong Kong, even madder than taking the piss out of Angus! As is said earlier we stayed on the 17th Floor of our building and Graeme Hedley and his wife lived one floor above us. Graeme's wife's parents had been out for a visit and they were having a going away party for them in their flat. All the Europeans were there with their partners and the Chinese lads who lived in our building were there as well. The layout of the flat was that the living room had the bathroom door of it and a small corridor up to the bedrooms. During the party we were all sat around the living room having a sing song and everyone would take a turn at singing or at least starting a song that everyone could join in. I went to the toilet and the window was open. I had a few drinks and had a look out the window and seen that one of the bedroom windows was open. I thought it would be a good idea to go out the toilet window along a small ledge about 2 inches wide

Watching training at the Happy Valley with Ryoden's Dutch coach Franz van Balkom

The Rydoden FC squad on the day before I left Hong Kong

while holding on to a drain pipe between the two windows and going in to the bedroom. This would leave no one in the locked toilet. As I emerged from the bedroom corridor, I was spotted by Driess Visser and he realised what I must have done but I put my finger to my lip to ask him not to say anything. I then proceeded to bang on the toilet door asking whoever was in there to hurry up as I needed a pee. Everyone was looking around to try and work out who was in the toilet and then they came to the door and were banging on it to try and find out who was in it. This was my cue to slip back to the bedroom out the window along the ledge and back in to the toilet. I then pulled my trousers around my ankles and opened the door asking why I can't have a shit in peace. The looks on everyone's faces when I opened the door was priceless. The next day people were reminding me what I had done and how dangerous it was. I must admit that I do have flashbacks to it and I realise that I must have been off my head. By a mile the silliest and stupidest thing I have ever done.

After we secured our place in the top division people thoughts started turning to the following season and I was told that the club would like me to stay, and I told them that I would like to stay. Duncan told me that they wanted him to stay but he had already decided that he was going to retire. He told me that he had been offered £20K to stay for another season. I asked him for advice on what I should ask for and he said that he thought I had done well and that I should ask for £10K. To be honest I would have been happy with half of that.

Due to an injury, I picked up in our second last game I asked if I could get away a week early so that I could have a holiday on the way back to the UK. My friend Gary Maitland had come out for the last month I was to be in Hong Kong and we decided to have a week in Thailand on the way back to Scotland. I therefore had to have my resigning talks with the club one week earlier. I went to Mr Tam's office. Mr Tam worked for Ryoden

My pal Gary and I at Victoria Peak in Hong Kong

and was the club representative or possibly secretary. He told me that there would be an increase in the weekly wage plus a new bonus system and increased expenses and that they wanted me to sign again and he had the paperwork ready for me to sign for another season. I asked him about a signing on fee and he asked what I was looking for and when I said £10K he burst out laughing and this annoyed me so I decided there and then that is what I wanted. When he refused, I said that I was happy with the new terms but that they should get back to me on the signing on fee and that we could agree on it when I came back after my break in Scotland. My existing contract was kept in place and I left for home via Thailand.

I was back in Scotland for a few weeks and was getting my weekly wage put in to my bank account every week and then one week it did not appear. I left it for a few days and then I got 5 weeks wages put in at once. I called Graeme Hedley to ask him if he knew what was happening and he told me that they had dissolved the team. We were told that the club no longer existed and that all contracts were being honoured so my 5 weeks wages were up until the official end of the contract I had. If I had signed my new contract, I would have got a whole year's payment. Some of the other lads had signed and came out of it well.

I was later told that allegedly one of the teams that had been relegated, South China, were one of the "big two" teams in Hong Kong and a plan was hatched to get them back up and for this to happen one of the top league teams had to disappear. There was a lot of money flying around Hong Kong then and Ryoden FC disappeared and South China FC came back in to the First Division. I wrote to the Hong Kong FA to ask them to alert teams that I would like to come back and play there, but apart from some interest from a team that paid their players part time wages there was no response as most teams had their allocation of foreigners.

My Hong Kong adventure came to an end, but I have so many memories of a fantastic time in my life.

So here I was, back in Scotland with no job and no football club.

Where to start?

Chapter 12

Inverness Thistle

So, here I am back in Scotland and living in Aberdeen with no club and no job.

I still had my room in Willie Skinner's flat in Brighton Place, Aberdeen and my preference was to find a job in Aberdeen. I tried for several opportunities in drawing offices in the Oil Industry but there were no openings at that time. I also spoke with some clubs about playing for them and managed to get some training facilities with Rosemount.

A report appeared in the Press & Journal that I had spoken to Brora Rangers and it said that I was happy to join them. This took me by surprise as I had not spoken to anyone at Brora. It transpired that the Brora Rangers manager had looked up the phone book and found a J Oliver in Fearn. This was my Uncle Jack's house and was where my cousin Jim Oliver lived. The Brora manager on getting an answer asked if he could speak to Jim Oliver and was put on to my cousin. He quickly realised what was up and said that he would be happy to sign on. When I got in touch with Brora to find out what was going on I quickly realised what had happened and apologised to Brora. I met my cousin in the pub a couple of weeks later and he was having a laugh about it, but I had the last laugh as he had put his name down on a scratch card that night and was not there when it was revealed that Jim Oliver was the winner - what else could I do but pocket the cash!

Around this time Jock MacDonald who was the Chairman of Inverness Thistle FC got in touch with me and said that he would like me to come and have a chat about joining them. He told me that they had a couple of players from the Aberdeen area Jim George and Charlie Duncan who trained in the Aberdeen area and only travelled North on match days. I remembered reading about Inverness Thistle being a great football playing team that played football how it should be played and I thought I might as well go and see what they had to say.

Thistle had a midweek match against Inverness rivals Clachnacuddin at Grant Street Park and Jock said that he would like me to play in this game. I agreed to come up and play as a Trialist. I was introduced to the Thistle Manager the legend that is Roshie Fraser. I was then introduced to the players in the dressing room. There were some great players in that team. The likes of Dave Milroy, Tichy and Brain Black, Mike Andrews and we had a sub outfield player who was to become a Highland Legend as a goalkeeper. I always say to Jim Calder that the first time I seen him as a centre forward I knew he would make a great goalkeeper.

It was a crisp autumn evening in the Highland capital and there was a noisy home crowd in what I later learned to be the Wine Shed. During the match I had a 50/50 challenge in the centre circle with Clach's up and coming big centre forward Duncan Shearer who went on to have a fantastic career. I came off the best in that tussle as Duncan got winded in the clash. The home fans were now on my case and it did not help when I shot Thistle in to the lead and ran over to give them a wave.

With Brian Fraser adding a second the score was 2-0 to us with about 10 mins to go when the ball went out for a Thistle throw in right in front of the Wine Shed. As I made my way over to take it I heard about 20 people clearing their throats and you would think it had started snowing as they let it all out!! I left the ball there. We won 2-0 and Jock took me back to the Thistle Social Club in Baron Taylor Street where we had signing talks. Jock did all the signing negotiations and had a reputation for being a bit of a task master and quite intimidating. I knew that I had had a big influence on the game that night and that I had played well. Scoring was a bonus so I was in a good position for asking for what I wanted. I told Jock how much I wanted to sign and he said "Our top player doesn't even get that" I told him that I wasn't interested in what anyone else gets as that is what I wanted and felt I was worth. To my amazement he took a roll of notes out of his pocket peeled some off and said there you go the forms are inside. I went in and signed without counting the money and I still don't know until this day if it was correct. Some former Thistle players told me that he used to give a few extra notes to see if you would own up to being over paid. I never checked. I was to have a good relationship with Jock as he knew that he couldn't intimidate me and I think he respected me for that. I was to have further dealings with him that backed this up.

So that was me sorted out with a club but still without a job. I enjoyed my journeys to Inverness with Goalkeeper Jim George and midfielder Charlie Duncan. I remembered playing against Charlie when he was at Peterhead and I was at Fraserburgh but I did not realise just how good he was until I played alongside him. If he had the ball you just needed to look at him and then make your run and invariably the ball would be there when you needed it there. A lot of players played the ball when they wanted to play it and more than often you had to abort your run to stay onside. Not with Charlie though it was on your toe when and where you needed it. Charlie went on to be an outstanding manager of Fraserburgh and a few generations of Brochers owe him a lot.

I was still looking for a job in Aberdeen but there was nothing of any

Inverness Thistle F.C. 1983-84
Back Row L to R: Murd Urquhart (trainer), Billy Sanderson, Billy Wilson, Mike Andrew, Jim George, Jim Calder, James Oliver & Brian Fraser
Front Row L to R: Gerry Scott, Alistair Black, Brian Black, Roshie Fraser (manager), Dave Milroy, Alan MacDonald & Colin Maclean

interest. As I was now in Inverness every second Saturday, I was starting to go home for weekends a bit more.

When I was at home one weekend a friend of mine Mitch McIlroy said to me that he could get me a start at the Nigg Fabrication Yard working for Highlands Fabricators as a Technical Clerk. I asked him to put my name forward and the following week he told me that I started on the Monday working in the same section as him.

This meant leaving Aberdeen and coming back to the Highlands to live. It also meant that I was able to attend the Inverness Thistle training at nights in Inverness. The Kessock Bridge that had been built in the years that I was away from the Highlands meant that the journey from Easter Ross to Inverness was much shorter.

I cleared all my possessions from Willie Skinner's flat and had a few farewell drinks with my friends from Aberdeen and headed back to my mother and fathers house in Hilton.

The football was going well and I was scoring a few goals for Thistle and I was enjoying it. At work there had been a problem with some of the welding on the Conoco TLP leg sections and all the welds had to be gouged out and re-done. This was a huge setback for the project and because the fault lay with the client, they asked Highlands Fabricators to get as many people on to the job as possible. They agreed to pay 10% on top of everyone's wages to get the job back on track. This meant longer hours and we were asked to work 7 x 12 hour shifts per week.

Due to this shift pattern, it was impossible to attend training and I shouldn't even have been playing the games however I was given dispensation to play on Saturdays. I noticed that I was however still getting paid for 7 x 12 hour shifts and brought it to the attention of my section leader. He said that it was a management decision to pay me that as they were charging the client for the full week. This however was brought up one week when Mitch took me aside and said that his Manager had said to him, "Tell Jim to stop scoring for Thistle as his name is in the Sunday Post scoring on Saturday when he was supposed to have been working on site."

I was unable to attend any training and gradually my fitness got to a stage where I was not fit to play and I would go to work instead. If Thistle needed me then I would ask for the day off but I appreciated that I would be used as a sub.

As the season petered out, I was not offered another contract and I don't blame the club as I was unable to train and had become very unfit.

As the project at Nigg neared completion we were all told that we would be getting paid off. My role there as a Technical Clerk was to provide the Welding Inspectors with their paperwork for the inspection. In the office next to me were some Draughtsmen who were responsible for pulling out

Inverness Derby - Thistle v Caledonian - showing concentration with Kevin Mann

the drawings and showing the Inspectors where on the rig the weld was located. The weld code is connected to the drawing number and makes it easy to find if you are a Draughtsman…which I was. I spoke with one of the Draughtsmen and he asked me how I knew how to read the drawings and I said that I was a Draughtsman and he asked me why I was working as a Tech Clerk as the Darughtsman's rate was almost double. He gave me the name of the agency that he worked for and the name of the person to speak to for future projects.

When the project finished it was around the end of May and the football season was winding up. With the redundancy package I got myself and my older cousin Derek Wood decided to have a trip round Europe.

I include this next period in my Inverness Thistle spell as I was to return to the club half way through the following season.

It turned out to be quite a trip and we had one or two games of football on our travels. First of all, we went to Greece and went to the South to a village called Tolo where Derek's parents had been the year before. They had made friends there and we rented out a small flat from them at very reasonable cost. We had a great time in the sun and drank quite a bit of ouzo.

I was also taking the opportunity to get myself fit again and would get out on the beach in the morning for a run. One morning while out running I bumped in to Valerie Singleton of Blue Peter fame walking along the beach. I stopped and had a walk and a chat with her but never got a Blue Peter Badge. A lovely friendly woman though whom we met several times after that in the local pubs.

When the locals found out that Derek and I played football they asked if we would like to play for them against a neighbouring village and we were up for it. The pitches were not made of grass but were a bit like the blaze that you get in some parks in Glasgow. They were not made for tackling on.

We are playing against this team and one of their players puts in a hefty challenge on Derek which ends up with Derek on the gravely surface and not a happy bunny. A couple of minutes later the same player is heading towards the touchline with the ball and I am thinking I will time it so I can take him out and make it look like a legitimate tackle. Just then Derek comes flying past me and nearly puts this guy over the fence and has totally wrecked him. The whole place erupts and there was a fair bit of pushing, shoving, jostling and cursing going on. Eventually the ref gets everyone calmed down and says it is a foul and I asked which way and it all started again!!

We played another game in Greece against some locals and I decided to play at the back for us as I did not fancy doing too much running due to having had several ouzos the night before. The other team were beating us 1-0 with a few minutes to go and one of their players was taunting me by saying that they were going to beat us. I picked up the ball and ran the whole length of the pitch beating about 4 men before rifling a left foot shot in to the far of top corner from the edge of the box. Without a doubt one of the best goals I have ever scored. I turned round and jogged all the way back behind our goals accepting my teammates congratulations and promptly threw up.

After eight weeks travelling Derek and I found ourselves back in London and Derek was going to meet some girl from Stevenage that he met in Corfu and I was heading off to Magaluf to meet the Aberdeen boys for two weeks.

I met up with a few of my former Montrose teammates in Magaluf and there was one of my former Rosslyn Sports teammates John Foote in the group as well. Stuart Beedie had left Montrose to play for St Johnstone and now was on the verge of a transfer to Dundee United. While we were out there, we met a few of the Dundee United players who were also on holiday and we found out that there was a waiter's team that were almost unbeatable, so we got our squad together to play them.

I had been injured on the beach the day before at volleyball so I said that I would be referee for the game. They found me a whistle and we got the game started. They were not a bad side but we had the likes of John Clark in our team plus a few other United starlets. They did however have a sweeper who was very good at the offside trap and he would come out and shout "offside!" and he was right most times. However, John Clark got the ball in his own half and made a run and slipped the ball through and kept running after it while the sweeper shouted for offside against the other player who was not interfering with play. John ran through and scored, something he was to become good at in Spain!

The Sweeper, who was also the captain of their team and as it transpired the owner of the bar where the team came from was fucking raging. He came running at me in a very threatening way and called me a cheat and that I was not to be the referee anymore. I took the whistle from around my neck and threw it on the ground. First game as a ref and I get sent off!!

I did however go over to our bench (I know I shouldn't say our bench after being referee) and grabbed a strip and made a substitution and you should have seen the look on the sweepers face when I came on and stood beside him. We won that game 5-1 and we were told that next time they would play their full team.

This next game was organised for a few days later and it was played at a small stadium and we again beat them 5-1. All of our outfield players had at least Highland League experience except for our Goalkeeper Tommy from Glasgow who was man of the Match with a string of great saves on a blaze type surface. The Sweeper was gracious in defeat this time and invited us back to his bar for a few drinks. I think the first one was free then he made a killing.

I returned to the Highlands and got in touch with Alan Houghton of Hi-Tec as they were the Draughting agency that I was given information about. Within a week they contacted me, and I had a short-term job at Cromarty Firth Engineering as a Draughtsman. When that was finished, I was offered another agency role with Hi-Tec working at the Ardersier Fabrication Yard and as this yard was on the other side of Inverness, I moved into a rented house with my cousin Graham who also worked at Ardersier.

I was now living in Inverness and able to attend training and started going along to some of the Thistle sessions to keep fit. I was not playing for anyone but enjoying getting fit again.

After New Year 1985 Thistle had a few injuries and picked up a few more after their first game in the Scottish Cup against Spartans from Edinburgh in Inverness which they drew. Roshie asked me if I would help them out by signing on so that I could play in the Scottish Cup. I said that I would love to and I signed a contract until the end of the season. I did not ask Jock for a signing on fee as I had had a good one before and felt I owed the club something.

As it happened, I was not able to play in the replay against Spartans as you had to be signed in time to play in the first game to be eligible to play in the replay. So, with the draw already made and Inverness Thistle or Spartans playing First Division Kilmarnock at home there was a lot at stake. Thankfully the lads managed to beat Spartans in Edinburgh in the replay which meant that we were at home to Killie in the next round. Our pitch was frozen when the tie was due to be played and the draw for the next round had taken place and it was a beauty. The winners of Inverness Thistle and Kilmarnock were drawn away to Celtic. When you are a small club there are two ties that you dream off to rake in the money and that is away to Rangers or Celtic.

So, with both teams knowing what the prize was we prepared for the game in Inverness. On the day of the game, it was a beautiful sunny day but the temperature the night before had been below freezing and the pitch was flat but solid. When we walked out on the park it was debateable whether the game would go ahead or not. I think a bit of pressure was put on the referee to play it by Kilmarnock as they would not like a return journey to Inverness through the week.

I also had a problem as I only had boots with Aluminium studs with me as my rubber soled boots were in my house less than a mile away. I went out to make an attempt to go and drive home for them but the crowds were gathering and it was impossible to get out. I asked around the dressing room if any of the lads had a spare pair of size 11 rubbers to no avail. It was then that I noticed Brian Fraser had trainer like shoes and I asked if I could try them out. Brian let me try them and while they were very tight, they at least could be used on the surface. So, with Brian's best shoes on I took the field to do battle with Killie. We had a brilliant performance that day as we ran out worthy winners 3-0 a score line which flattered Kilmarnock. I had a shot going in to the top corner which the goalie tipped over the bar and from the resultant corner Mike Andrew nodded down for Dave Milroy to score. Two second half goals from Graham Hay and Brian Fraser sealed a fantastic win and kicked off a night of celebrations in Inverness.

The Kilmarnock fans showed their disgust with the team by throwing their scarves on to the back of the net on their way out of the ground. Indeed, several supporters gathered outside the main stand demanding resignations from the Board of Directors and Management. We had some night and a Kilmarnock Supporter gave me his scarf which I have kept as a souvenir.

The next day I was asked to play for Dillinger's in a friendly match against another pub team from Inverness. I was still half cut from the night before and we were getting beat 2-1 with about 5 mins to go when one of their team said to me…a bit of a comedown for you after yesterday's result. 5 mins and two goals from me later and we had won 3-2. I think I played better when people riled me. Should have got riled before going out on the pitch!!

So, the scene was set for us that we were heading to Parkhead to take on the mighty Celtic. There was a media frenzy in Inverness that week and the TV cameras and Archie MacPherson and his famous jacket turned up at Kingsmills. We were also told that Celtic v Inverness Thistle was to be the featured match on Sportscene that Saturday. This was fantastic news for the club as it would add more revenue to the share of the gate money that we would get from Celtic.

I can't recall the person's name, but he was originally from Inverness and was in the Management team at the Central Hotel in Glasgow. The Hotel

Picture special page 43

JOY BOYS . . . Jim Oliver rushes over to congratulate Davie Milroy after the centre half had shot Thistle into the lead nine minutes from half time last Saturday, which set the Kingsmills men up for the most famous result in their history. Gordon Hay headed the second in 81 minutes after lobbing keeper McCulloch, then substitute Brian Fraser scored with virtually his first touch of the ball when he latched on to an Oliver cross-cum-shot invited the Inverness Thistle team to stay there on the Friday and Saturday nights while down to play the game. This was a shrewd move by the Hotel as hundreds of Thistle supporters were coming down to stay and they were given special rates to stay in the hotel. There was a party atmosphere in the Hotel on the Friday night as the excitement rose for the game the following day. I think that there were some nerves from the younger lads at potentially being hammered and having it shown on TV at night.

When we arrived at the hotel, we all headed up to our rooms and I was sharing with Billy Sanderson. Billy was a fireman and I did not know him all that well personally but we had a good chat before we went down for our tea. I was about last to come in to the restaurant and sat beside Roshie (the Manager) and Brian Fraser. When the waitress came and asked me what I would like to drink while I was waiting for my food, I said I would like a pint of lager. The room fell silent as everyone else was on soft drinks. I said that I needed one to calm me down and Roshie said it was OK for everyone to have only one alcoholic drink.

We mixed with the fans who were not restricted to the one drink and they were having a great time. Around this time, we found out what our bonus was for beating Kilmarnock in the previous round and bearing in mind what the club were going to collect the following day it was very poor. A delegation of the older players insisted that we be given a better deal than what was given and there was talk of a boycott of the game the next day. I won't divulge who the ringleader was but it ended up with us getting an extra £100 per person. I don't think Jock was too pleased at this mini revolt and the ring leader was dealt with in the coming months.

On the morning of the match, we had a warmup session at Lesser Hampden where we did a bit of stretching and some light running then it was back to the hotel for a light lunch. A few of the boys hit the bookies and I put a bet on us getting a goal in the game. This was before the authorities frowned upon players and officials betting on games they were involved in.

Several of the Thistle fans were just rising as we were getting ready to get the bus to Parkhead. When we got there, you could sense some of the players were a bit nervous and we tried to get a bit of crack going on the bus by waving to the Celtic fans as we approached the stadium. It looked like they were thinking their team were going to score 2 by the hand signals they were giving us. When we got to the ground, we walked out on to the pitch in brilliant sunshine, but it was freezing, and the park was every bit as hard as the Kingsmills pitch was against Kilmarnock.

I met my former Dundee United team mate Tom McAdam who had joined Celtic and we had a wee chat about how things had gone for each of us from our days at United. Tom had joined United from Dumbarton as a centre forward and had been converted in to a centre half. We realised that we were going to be in direct opposition to each other if we were both picked.

Souvenir of the game, kept in my memory box

We got called in by Roshie and went to the away dressing room and the team was named. It was the same 13 that were involved for the game with Kilmarnock. The club had signed a youngster from Inverness Caley in between the ties and it was thought that he might be taken in to the team. Roshie chose to be loyal and stick with the guys who had done so well against Killie. This meant that Charlie Christie had to wait to begin his fantastic career at Inverness Thistle.

The Referee popped in the Celtic team lines and their team was Peter Latchford, William McStay, Daniel McGrain, Peter Grant, Thomas McAdam, Pierce O'Leary, David Provan, Paul McStay, Maurice Johnstone, Murdo MacLeod, Francis McGarvey with Alan McInally and Owen Archdeacon the subs.

I know this because I popped the teamlines in to my jacket and still have them until this day. I was thinking of appealing for a replay as they had spelt Maurice Johnston's name wrong.

The Thistle lads who lined up that day to take on this star-studded array of talent was Les Fridge, Billy Skinner, Billy Wilson, Mike Andrew, Dave Milroy, Billy Sanderson, Graham Hay, Colin MacLean, Alistair (Tichy) Black, Alan MacDonald and Jim Oliver with Brian Fraser and Jimmy Calder the subs.

After the problems with footwear against Kilmarnock I had packed my trainers along with my rubber soled boots. After trying out both I thought that the trainers were best suited for the type of surface. The trainers were however white and Archie MacPherson gave them a mention in the commentary on Sportscene at night.

So with Tom McAdam being named in their team we faced up to each other. The first high ball that came up to me Tom made his intentions clear by coming straight through me to get the ball. The next time one came up I got my own back on him with a bit of a lunge. We had a good battle and

4:39 / 29:04

Sportscene highlights - moments after missing a chance against Celtic

kept it fairly sporting for the rest of the game.

After about 5 minutes the ball broke from a throw in and Tichy Black tried to control the ball which had bounced quite high on the hard surface only to be poleaxed by a kick in the ribs from Danny McGrain who arrived quite late. Tichy took a sore one and McGrain was leaning over him asking him if he was OK and the referee was there as well when Thistle Trainer Murdy Urquhart arrived on the scene and punched McGrain in the ribs to get past him to treat Tichy. This would go down in folklore in Inverness as Murdy was admonished by the referee for his abrupt entrance to the fray. The look on McGrain's face at the time was priceless.

A few minutes later came the big moment with the score still 0-0. The ball was on the right wing and a Celtic player and a Thistle player went for it with the Thistle player getting there just ahead of him. The ball came out nicely and was coming towards the box. I ran forward and chested it down and got in to the box and next thing I was looking at getting a shot at goals. My excuse is that the ball bounced higher than normal from the hard surface and I never made a good connection on it and skewed the ball wide of the far post. This moment has been played back in my mind many times and I have also been reminded of it many, many times by Thistle supporters, players and basically anyone who wanted to wind me up. My reply to them is that I was the only player with the skill and pace to get past the Celtic back line that day.

Celtic went straight up the park and McGarvey scored to put Celtic 1-0 up. Roshie tells everyone that I cost him Europe that day as Celtic did the double that year and if we had beaten Celtic, we would have won the Cup. I think Roshie is still on drugs.

We put in a hard shift that day and eventually got beat 6-0 with Celtic getting two very late goals which disappointed us. If we had only been beaten 4-0 then that would have been a fairer reflection on the game.

At the end the Celtic fans started shouting "Thistle, Thistle" and gave us a round of applause for the efforts that we put in that day. Little did the Celtic fans know that two of our squad would be back several years later to pull off one of the Scottish Cup's biggest shocks.

Charlie Christie would be Man of the Match that night and one of our outfield substitutes Jimmy Calder would have the game of his life in goals in the Inverness Caledonian Thistle FC "SupercaleygoballisticCelticareatrocious" game.

With the game over it was now time for us to drown our sorrows and we all went back to the Central Hotel where the drink was already flowing. There was a huge Highland Party there that night as Players, Officials and Fans mixed throughout the Hotel.

Brian McGinlay who was one of the top Referee's in Scotland at the time had been referee at the Rangers v Dundee cup tie at Ibrox that day. Brian had a friendship with the Thistle Officials as he was the referee who was in charge of the Scottish Cup game against Falkirk that had the record number of postponements. Brian had come to the Hotel to meet the Thistle officials and have a few drams with them. He ended up coming to the Horseshoe Bar with us and I noticed that he had a tie on with the Olympic logo on it. I told him that I liked his tie and that I wanted it. He said I got this tie for officiating at the Olympic games and that it was not available. I said to him will you take it off or will I take it off you? He was so pissed that within 30 seconds I was the proud wearer of an Olympic tie. Just then I got a shout from some girls at a table and they were girls from Glasgow that I had met in Magaluf the year before. It was a manic night in the Horseshoe Bar and when I got back to the Central Hotel with a large bag of crisps, I was well oiled. Tichy Black grabbed my bag of crisps and started running down the corridor with them. Normally Tichy would leave me for dead but when food is involved it was different and I caught up with him and rugby tackled him. The result was that the bag burst and there were crisps everywhere. Not sure what time I decided to call it a day but when I got in to my room there was someone in my bed. I grabbed the person by the ankles and started pulling them off the bed. Just as their head was coming off the end of the bed they woke up. It was Mike Andrews' brother Robin who had decided to crash out and just grab someone bed. He slept on the floor.

The next morning was like a scene from a disaster movie as people were making their way down for breakfast still half cut. Some of us decided to have a few beers just to keep the hangover away.

Later on, as we were making our way back to Inverness on the bus I mentioned to Roshie that I thought the training could do with some variety. Jock in his usual gruff voice said what is wrong with the current training? I said that to be honest it was boring and that we needed more time on actual football training instead of just running. I said why don't you let myself or Brian Black have a go at taking the training. Brian had

Match programme v Celtic

THE SCOTTISH FOOTBALL ASSOCIATION LTD.

PATRON: HER MAJESTY THE QUEEN

SECRETARY
E. WALKER

ADDRESS ALL CORRESPONDENCE
TO "THE SECRETARY"   Our Reference _____

**6 PARK GARDENS,
GLASGOW G3 7YF**

_____ CELTIC _____ v. _____ INVERNESS THISTLE F.C. _____

At _____ Celtic Park, Glasgow. _____ on _____ Saturday, 16th FEBRUARY, 1985.

In the _____ Fourth _____ round of the _____ SCOTTISH CUP _____ Kick-off _____ 3p.m.

Details of team representing _____ CELTIC _____ F.C.

No.	Name (Christian Name and Surname)	Address
1	Peter Latchford	The Old Bakery, Ogstone Place, Inverkip.
2	William McStay	3 Cameron Path, Larkhall.
3	Daniel McGrain	16 Durness Avenue, Boclair, Bearsden.
4	Peter Grant	115 Gibb Street, Chapelhall, Airdrie.
5	Thomas McAdam	28 Ardlui Gardens, Milngavie.
6	Pierce O'Leary	c/o Grosvenor Hotel, Glasgow.
7	David Provan	23 Leeburn Avenue, Houston.
8	Paul McStay	3 Cameron Path, Larkhall.
9	Maurice Johnstone	18 Burnbroom Gardens, Mount Vernon.
10	Murdo MacLeod	20 Duchess Park, Helensburgh.
11	Francis McGarvey	77 Menock Road, Glasgow.
12	Alan McInally	5 Oswald Court, Ayr.
13	Owen Archdeacon	12 Mossside Avenue, Port Glasgow.

Club Secretary or
Accredited Official _____

Result _____ CELTIC _____ F.C. _____ goals

_____ INVERNESS THISTLE _____ F.C. _____ goals

Referee _____

SFA Challenge Cups – Rule No. 41(a) – "Not later than thirty minutes before the start of the match, each club shall hand to the referee, a list, and to its opponent, a duplicate, both of which shall be signed by the Secretary or other accredited official, of the proper names and addresses of the players in its team and of such substitutes as are permitted, on forms provided by the Association. (b) Within three days thereafter (Sunday excluded) the referee shall send to the Secretary of the Association, the lists which were handed to him, which he shall also sign, and on which he shall intimate the result, and which substitute or substitutes played in th t match".

Celtic team lines from the day which I had framed and saved

been doing some coaching and was keen to get more involved. I had been at several different clubs and found the training at Thistle to be more suited to training required to be a runner.

Jock did not like this as the training was mostly done by his friend Murdy. I was soon to find out how much he did not like this as I was dropped from the squad the following week and only played a few more times for Thistle that season. One of the games was as a sub against Caley in the North of Scotland Cup Final at Grant Street where we won 1-0 through a Colin MacLean goal.

I was, however, to be vindicated about the training regime at Thistle as Brian Black became the Manager soon after this and he changed the training. A couple of years later I was asked by Brian to run their second team and I will come on to that later.

So that was the end of this stint at Kingsmills and as a free agent at the end of the season I did not know what was coming next.

Chapter 13

Rothes

It was to be another season starting without a team, but I wasn't too bothered as I had been playing some football in the summer. By this time, I was back working long hours at Nigg in the Drawing office and it was difficult to get to training on a regular basis. I think I had done a few sessions with Caley but I could see I was a mile off the fitness and I would struggle to get there, I had offers from Brora and Nairn but I was quite happy being able to go to games I wanted to see so turned them down.

One of my drinking buddies in Inverness, John MacDonald, better known as Johnny Mac, had left Inverness Caley and had joined Rothes and I met him on Saturday nights after he got back from their games. He told me that it was a great wee club to play for and it was good fun after the games as well. The Manager was Ray Bernardi who lived in Inverness and John said I should have a word with him but I wasn't too bothered about it.

I was living in a rented house on Old Edinburgh Road with my cousin Graham and a Kiwi called Grant Suddaby (whom we nicknamed Oz much to his annoyance). Most Saturday nights there was a party back at the house and this particular weekend Johnny Mac had invited a few of the Rothes lads through to Inverness for a night out. They all turned up at the party and soon we were all in the kitchen and John had obviously had a word with them all about putting a bit of pressure on me to come and join the club.

A number of the group were Aberdeen FC young professionals who had been loaned out to Rothes. Amongst them were Stevie King, Scott Harvie, Scott Brown and Gary Riddell. Gary was to collapse and die a few years later while doing a fundraising run while he was at Dunfermline Athletic FC. A lovely guy taken far too young.

We were all in the kitchen and they were all saying to me how great a club Rothes were and that I should come and join them. I grabbed a bottle of Vodka and poured a large drink for each of them and myself. There was to be no mixers in the Vodka as that was how Johnny Mac and I were drinking ours at that time.

I told them that if they could all down their drink in a oner I would sign for them. I downed mine followed by Johnny Mac and then we looked on as the others somehow managed to get their drink down their throats. It was left then for Stevie King to down his for me to sign for Rothes. You could tell that he did not fancy the task ahead of him. After quite a bit of cajoling from his team mates he went for it and the Vodka went down in about 2.5 seconds and then came up in about 1.5 seconds. It was however deemed to have been downed and the next task was for John to arrange for me to meet the Manager. I met Raymond and I signed on for the rest of the season.

I can't recall my first game for Rothes but there were some excellent players there at the time. Players like Dave Simpson, Derek Thomson, Mike Ritchie, Colin Tweedie, Gary Johnston and the aforementioned young lads from Aberdeen. From Inverness we had three former Caley lads in John, Derek Dewar and Robbie Baxter. Dave Simpson and Derek Thomson are still involved at the club in Committee roles. There was the nucleus of a good side.

I was still struggling to get to training but was doing some running to get fitter and got a few goals to help us get good results away to amongst others Elgin City, Inverness Thistle and Forres Mechanics who were all top teams at the time. I also scored at home against my former team Fraserburgh and then we had a game at home against Fort William.

As there was no dedicated Free Kick taker at the club it was usually the person who grabbed the ball first who took it. We got a direct free kick about 25 yards out and Gary Riddell got to the ball first. There was a few of them over the ball and eventually Gary convinced everyone that he should hit it.

I had kept out of the melee of players fighting over the ball and was standing about 10 yards back. Gary carefully placed the ball and started walking backwards to prepare his run up to the ball. This was my cue and I ran past him and hit one of my hardest shots I ever hit which was still rising as it hit the back of the net. The Fort goalkeeper never even moved as I turned to celebrate and take the plaudits from the home supporters, I could hear Gary running after me and shouting "You b*****d, that was my freekick!" In the Social Club afterwards Henrik Madej, the Fort William manager, came up to me and said that two of the best goals he had ever seen were scored by me against Fort William. The first was a volley from the edge of the 18-yard box straight from a corner for Balintore in the North Caledonian League and the freekick that day was the other.

I couldn't wait to see the report in the Sunday Post the next day to see how the free kick was reported. To my dismay and Johnny Mac's delight the report said "from a free kick awarded just outside the box Oliver found the net". He always brings that quote up if ever I mention the free kick.

Ray was unable to put in the time he needed to take the club on further and he decided to resign. The new manager was unveiled and it was the former Inverness Thistle player Johnny Cowie. Johnny was a tremendous goalscorer for Thistle in the early 70's and was highly respected as a player for his history in the game. He was also a gentleman.

It was coming up to the end of the season and we had been stringing a few good results together even though we were in the bottom half of the league. Back in those days there was a Sunday Post Team of the Month which was picked by their reporter Rodwill Clyne. Rod was another absolute legend of the Highland League and we knew that he used to enjoy a dram in the Red Lion in Auldearn. On our way home after another home win, we decided to call in to the Red Lion and sure enough Rodwill was there. We had a discussion about how we thought that we must be in the running for the Team of the Month award even though Caley had won all their games! Our reasoning was that Caley were expected to win while we were not and we had 3 wins and a draw against their 3 wins. I think we made a good argument as about 2 hours later we left a well filled up Rodwill agreeing with us that Rothes should get the award. We lost our last game and then the next day we were awarded Team of the Month to the surprise of many but not us.

The journeys down to Rothes from Inverness were usually in my car as it was the one best suited for 4 people. I was working at Nigg in the Oil Industry and had got myself a BMW 316 which was a really nice car at the time. The only problem I had was that if I took the car then I could not have a drink. It was then that I discovered the merits of shared driving. I got the car insured so that Derek Dewar was covered to drive it and we shared the driving. I drove down and he drove home. I also said to Derek he could take the car home after dropping us off in town and he could get it back to me in time for me to get to work on Mondays. Derek loved driving around in it on Sundays while I wasn't fit to drive so it worked out well for everyone.

The last thing that I did as a Rothes player was to go on the end of Season trip to Shetland. This was to be an epic journey and a whole book could be written about that weekend alone. Johnny Mac, Robbie Baxter, Andy Campbell from Newtonmore and myself arranged to meet up in the Moray Bar a couple of hours before our train was due to go. Derek Dewar could not get the time off work and was catching a later train.

We had a wee carry out for the train as well and by the time we arrived in Aberdeen we had a wee glow about us and Andy and Robbie were starting to feel the pace. We walked from the Station up to Ma Camerons and had a few there and then we started to make our way down to the P&O Ferry Terminal to catch the overnight sailing to Lerwick.

Across from the Ferry Terminal there was a bar and we went in there for a few more while we waited for the boarding time. Eventually it was time to make our way to the Terminal and as John and I crossed the road we did not notice that Robbie had fallen on the road and we both fell over him. As all 3 of us were trying to get up as the official Rothes bus pulled in to the car park. God knows what the guys must have been thinking about what was happening.

Once we were all on board Robbie and I went looking for a bar and we found one where a member of the crew was preparing for the trip ahead. We asked if we could have 2 pints of lager.

The barman replied in a very effeminate voice, "We can't serve you until we leave the harbour."

Robbie said to him "Come on you p**f, give us a drink!"

The barman said, "That's it, you're barred."

I tried to plead on Robbie's behalf, but the barman was having none of it. Eventually I said to him, "If you give us a drink, I will give you a kiss"

The barman said, "That's it, the two of you are barred."

We had not even untied from the harbour and we were both barred.

Just as well there was more than one bar on board. We stayed up most of the night having a few beers and a sing song with the band that were on the ship. We were staying on the ship while it was berthed in Lerwick and when we woke up in the morning after about 3 hours sleep we were tied to the harbour in Lerwick.

We had 2 games to play while we were there. The first was a game against a team called Whitedale to officially open Storm Park their new pitch. We were to find out the next day why it was called Storm Park. The kick off for this game was 6.30pm to allow us some time to rest (and sober up) after our journey. I can't recall much about the game, but it was played in good conditions and we won 3-1 despite a number of our team being under the weather.

After the game we were invited to a reception where we proceeded to top ourselves up from the night before and eventually most of us made our way back to the boat around 2.00am. Johnny Cowie had given us all information of what time we needed to be ready to leave for the second game and also what time we need to be at the park if we missed the bus. As it was a number of players had not made it back to the boat and we had to leave without them. When we got to Storm Park for the 12 noon kick off the other players were there.

We were all feeling a bit tired and worn out after the exploits of the previous couple of days and the wind was getting up. In addition to this we were playing the Island Select and I think they may all have been tucked up in their beds the night before.

The team was announced and we went outside. By this time there was a howling gale blowing straight down the pitch and we had to play against it in the first half. Our goalkeeper Mike Ritchie, who went on to become a Highland League referee, could not get his goal kicks to clear the 18-yard box such was the power of the wind. I ended up taking them but could only get them about 30 yards up the park. The first half was an absolute onslaught by the Island team and we could hardly get over the half way line. We did incredibly well to keep the score to 1-0 at half time for the Islanders.

We did, however, lose our skipper in the first half as Derek Dewar was taken off by the Manager after about 10 mins. We had got a free kick just outside their box after 5 mins and Derek, although still pissed insisted on taking it, as he ran up to kick the ball he fell over and landed on top of the ball. It was a very tired team that trudged in at half time.

We were, however, buoyed by the fact that we now had the wind behind us this half. We were however in for a shock. When we got out of the dressing room and back on to the pitch there was not a breath of wind!! It was as if someone had switched off a giant fan.

We started the second half and were soon on top and a "cross" from Derek Thomson got us back level. Then against the run of play the Islanders took the lead again when Derek Leask, whom I was to meet on business many years later, playing his first game for the Island Select put them 2-1 up. With us entering the last minute it looked like we were going to suffer a

**The Whitedale FC and Rothes FC teams and match officials
line up for a photo**

defeat when we were awarded a throw in about 30 yards out. I had a long throw in so we put everyone in the box and I launched it in. A few people went for it and all missed it and it bounced on the hard ground and was going in the net when the goalie tried to save it and pushed it in to his own net. If he had left it then it would not have been allowed as you can't score direct from a throw in.

The whistle went minutes after this and we all got in to the dressing room and collapsed. This lasted until a crate of beer was put in to our dressing room and that was it started again. As we were getting changed Derek Dewar asked Johnny Cowie why he had taken him off after 10 mins and Johnny said because the ball had not gone out for 5 mins. You would have been off earlier if it had. We had a great few hours with the Shetland lads until it was time to go and get our ferry back to Aberdeen in the early evening.

Once more we were up most of the night and then we still had to get back to Inverness. We eventually finished about 6.00pm on the Monday in Reflections in Inverness. Derek Dewar had found a fence post in Shetland that someone had drawn a fish face on and he named it Sammy the Swordfish and he was the last to leave Reflections. What a trip and what we refer to as the Rothes undefeated oversees adventure.

On the trip with us was a young man who was cutting his teeth in the Highland League as a member of the committee. He was to go on to become a top referee both in Highland league and Scottish League circles. He is now the General Manager of Peterhead FC and I am sure Martin Johnston learnt a few things on that trip.

WHITEDALE FOOTBALL CLUB

OFFICIAL OPENING
OF STROM PARK

Souvenir Programme

WHITEDALE	V	ROTHES
FC		FC

on SATURDAY, 17th May, 1986
Kick-Off 6.30 pm

ROTHES FC v SHETLAND XI

on SUNDAY, 18th May, 1986
Kick-Off 11.00 am

Price £1.00

Chapter 14

Clachnacuddin

I had enjoyed my time with Rothes but I wanted to get a team closer to Inverness and I was delighted to be contacted by Dave Christie the new manager at Inverness Clachnacuddin FC. The Lilywhites had a great history in the Highland League but had been struggling for a few years. Dave was a former Captain of all three of the Inverness teams and was a highly respected person in the football family in the Highland Capital. Dave had approached Derek Dewar and asked him if he wanted to sign for Clach and Derek had suggested that he also ask Johnny Mac, Robbie and myself. John and I joined but Robbie decided that he wanted to leave Inverness and he headed down to London to work.

So, I was now a Lilywhite and it was to be the beginning of a long link with the club over a few different spells. Dave Christie decided that my best position for the team was to be at the back but that I was also available to play up front if required. I was quite happy to play anywhere on the park as long as I was getting a game. I had no real preference over which foot I kicked the ball with as I had always been two footed from my days in primary school. I had been right footed but on breaking my big toe in my right foot it was either learn to kick with the left or not play. Quite a drastic way to go about learning to kick with your weaker foot but it worked out well for me.

We had a good squad of players which included the likes of Darren MacLean, Graeme Bennett, Ally Jappy. Mike Paul, Derek Wright, Alan MacQueen and Hamish Morrison. Mike Paul and myself paired up as central defenders and we switched between centre half and sweeper to cover each other. Mike like myself liked to go on runs up the park and it was important that we spoke to the midfield about covering when the other went on walk about.

At that time both Inverness Caledonian and Inverness Thistle were very strong teams and Clach were the third team in Inverness. We did however have a fanatical fan base that were resident in the Wine Shed. From having played against Clach many times for other teams it was good to have these guys behind me for a change. They were, however, quick to remind you if you were not at your best and sometimes, they were harder on their own players!

We had an okay season and finished lower mid table. This was the year that I got married and I recall my father-in-law stating on my wedding day that I could not be held responsible for a 4-1 defeat at home to Fort William that day. The season was quite uneventful and as it drew to a close, we were looking forward to the following season. Dave Christie decided that he did not wish to continue as manager and the hunt was on for a new manager during the close season.

The news that the Clachnacuddin board had appointed John Beaton as manager and former Clach manager Brian Mackay as his assistant was welcomed by all the players. John was involved in youth football in Inverness for many years and was a much-respected Coach and Trainer. Brian was a former manager who brought a steady hand to the club.

I was invited down to the club to speak with them and they told me that they would like to resign me but they did not think that they could afford me. I said to them that they did not know what I was looking for so how could they possibly tell whether I was too expensive. When they asked me what I wanted I think they were both shocked as I told them that I was not looking for anything to sign on. I told them that I was pleased to see them at the club and that I wanted to be part of what they were going to do at the club. They were both delighted and I signed there and then for no signing on fee. About three days later they resigned after a disagreement with the board as to what direction they wanted to take the club. This must have been the shortest managerial stint in the club's history. Still, I was now a signed player as were several others.

We were all wondering who the next manager would be, and a few names were being bandied around. When the new manager was revealed by Chairman Dougie Rodgers most of us had never heard of him before. In came Stuart Morrison who was the owner of the Royal Hotel in Cromarty. He had been managing the Cromarty team in the Ross-shire Amateur league during the summer and his name was mentioned to Dougie. Stuart's training was different, and I recall climbing up the canal banks with Mike Paul on my back. It must have been worse for Mike when it was his turn to carry me.

Several of the better younger players had been approached by either Thistle, Caley or Elgin City and we had an older team than in the previous season. Stuart took in some of his players from Cromarty and others whom they had played against in the Amateur leagues. Overall, the team got older, and we lost the quality that the younger players had.

Stuart asked me to be the captain of the team and I was delighted to take this on. As a young kid growing up, I was always captain of the school teams and the Under 16 teams that I played in and it always spurred me on to play better. The team struggled at the beginning of the season and then Stuart couldn't make it to training and he asked me as captain if I would

Winning their duel with Barclay and Stephen of Buckie Thistle. Looking on are John MacDonald, Alan McQueen and Gary Whyte.

Clachnacuddin F.C. 1987-88
Back Row L to R: Stuart Morrison (manager), Gavin Dearie, George Cowie, Bob MacLean, Martin Hill, James Oliver, Derek Rudkin, John MacDonald, Mike Paul, George Stewart & Andy Campbell
Front Row L to R: Kenny Milne, Ron Murray, Andy Gilchrist, Andy Gillan, Robbie Lowe, Alan Clark, Charlie Innes & John Bateson

take the training. I started to take the training and I quite enjoyed it as I got to do all the things I liked doing, which mostly involved the ball.

I had never bought in to the SFA coaching scene as I thought what is the sense of everyone going to the same place to learn how to attack and how to defend. Surely if you have something that you can surprise teams with it is an advantage to you. I think the rest of the guys were also enjoying the new training. We did a lot with the ball but built in to it there was a lot of running and physical effort which increased the overall fitness of the team. After a couple of months of doing this and Stuart appearing less and less at training the Board decided to dispense with his services. I was asked if I would temporarily take on the role of selecting the team until they found a new manager. I said I was happy to take it on as I knew I was going to be playing! This went on for a few weeks and I don't think they were able to find anyone willing to take on the Managers job so they asked me if I would become their Player Manager. I had never thought about getting in to Management or indeed Coaching a team but It felt right at the time and I said yes.

The new Chairman was a local man called Willie MacLennan who was well known in the Merkinch area of town where Clach are situated. Willie told me that the club were struggling financially and that hard times were ahead. At that time the club had a Social Club that was always busy at weekends and owned a large area of land where the Main Stand and the two terraces either side of it were located.

One of my former team mates at Dundee United was Walter Smith and he was now at Ibrox as Assistant Manager to Graeme Souness. Walter used to pick me up in the mornings in Broughty Ferry and take me in to training in his Triumph Toledo. Walter was one of the Senior Pros and was just starting out on his coaching career at the time and he and Archie Knox were usually put in charge of running the Reserve side. I had always got on well with Walter and decided to make contact with him to see if he could get Rangers to come and play us to raise some much-needed funds for the team.

I was delighted when he agreed to do this and we set about finding a suitable date. A date of Sunday April 10th 1988 was picked and local journalist Dave Love was to uncover that it was exactly 100 years on from when Rangers became the first ever Senior Club to visit the Highlands. With that game to look forward to the players had a spring in their step.

In the run up to the game against Rangers I had several meetings with the Council with regards to how many people we could get in to the game. The perimeter railing around the park was not in very good condition and it was causing the Council concerns. I spoke to my father and my brother who

THE
RANGERS
FOOTBALL CLUB plc
Founded 1873

23rd January 1988

Jim Oliver Esq.,
c/o Clacknacuddin F.C.,
Grant St. Park,
INVERNESS.

Dear Jim,

Many thanks for your recent letter regarding the financial difficulties which your Club unfortunately find themselves in at the moment.

We will be delighted to help in any way we can and pleased to send a Team north before the end of the Season. Perhaps you can forward some dates which would be suitable during March and April.

Normally at the start of the new Season, we send our Reserve Team, including one or two first team players, to the North of Scotland for one or two matches. We would be pleased to arrange a match at that time also if this would be of assistance to you.

I look forward to hearing from you.

Yours sincerely,

WALTER SMITH
Assistant Manager

P.S. James, if you are still playing as well as managing then I might make a comeback that night

A letter from my former teammate and friend Walter Smith - with personal note were both bricklayers and asked them if they could build a new perimeter wall around the pitch for us. Along with the help of a former team mate at Invergordon, Alan Stainke, they proceeded to build a new wall on 3 sides of the ground. They did all this work for free and we got the blocks donated by a local company. As they were completing the last section they ran out of cement and they reckoned that one maybe two bags would be sufficient. I went in to the social club and asked if anyone knew where I could get some bags of cement. A lad sitting at the bar who had had a few drinks said that he could get me a bag of cement which should be enough to finish the job but it would cost me a bottle of vodka. Wanting to get the job done I agreed and he left to get it. About 20 minutes later the same guy comes around the corner driving a forklift with a 1-ton bag of cement hanging from the forks. I never did find out that guy's name and it was probably better that I didn't know it!

The weekend of the game against Rangers we were due to be playing Elgin City at home in the Highland League. The league did not want the game postponed and we wanted to keep the pitch in a good condition for the Sunday game. We approached Nairn County and asked if we could play the game at Station Park. As I wanted to give the bulk of the players who had been loyal to the club the prestige of playing against a team such as Rangers, we asked a few players to guest for us as trialists on the Saturday. I went to my home village and asked 4 of their players to come and play for us. The guys I asked were Graham Skinner, Gordon Skinner, Gordon Lowe and Robert Allan. Only Robert had played Highland League before at Brora but all 4 were stand outs as we held a very strong Elgin City team to a 2-2 draw.

The game against Rangers drew a large crowd and it was reported that 4500 attended the game but I am pretty sure that there was more than this. The game was a very closely fought affair with Rangers obviously having

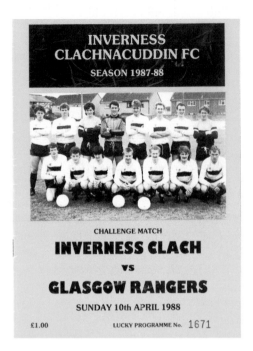

SHAKE ON IT . . . Clach player-manager Jim Oliver and Rangers captain Stuart Munro exchange pennants before the match.

Left: Welcoming Rangers and Gavin Dearie practising for being man in the middle. Right: Matchday souvenir programme

the lion's share of possession. 3 times we came back from a goal down before Rangers won the game 4-3 with a goal with 10 minutes to go. I was very proud of our guys as some of them had played the whole game the day before against Elgin City and they were up against full time professionals on the Sunday. I managed to play for 75 minutes myself and scored our 3rd equaliser in the 71st minute.

It was a great occasion and the Rangers group joined us in the Social Club for a few drinks and a bite to eat before heading back to Glasgow. While they were there the Deputy Provost for Inverness, Mr MacKenzie, made a speech and thanked Rangers for coming to help Clach in their hour of need. A slightly inebriated Mr MacKenzie then added "If Rangers ever find their selves in the same situation, then I am sure that Clach would come and help them"

When Rangers went in to administration I wondered how they would have felt about Clach offering to come to Ibrox for a fundraiser?

After the excitement of the Rangers game, it was back to the Highland League. We had mixed fortunes for the rest of the season as the team were capable of putting some good performances together. We became more difficult to beat and again finished in mid table.

We were however to play a crucial role in Inverness Caledonian winning the league on points from a strong Buckie Thistle team. All other games had been played in the Highland league except for the Clach v Buckie Thistle game. This was to be played on a Wednesday night at Grant Street Park. Buckie would go level on points with Caley if they won the game and if they won it by more than 7 goals, they would be Highland League Champions. Dave Watson the Buckie manager was keeping a positive mind on the game and knew that if his team got a good start that anything was possible. As we had suffered a 10-2 defeat away to Keith that season

Tussling with Derek Ferguson of Rangers F.C.

185

Celebrating scoring to make it 3-3

then it was possible for us to lose by 8 goals!

There was a big contingent of Caley fans at the game that night and several of their players were also watching from the grassy banks on the far side of the pitch. We received several messages of support from the Blue side of Inverness. We knew that Buckie would start like a whirlwind and but for some poor finishing and some fantastic saves by Clach goalkeeper Derek Rudkin they could have been 4-0 up in the first 20 minutes.

They eventually took the lead with a header after about 25 minutes and this seemed to settle us somehow as we started to play the ball around. Former Caley player Robbie Williamson scored a great equaliser for us just before half time and we came in level. Robbie was a local Merkinch lad and was not getting a game at Caley and I approached Caley Manager Peter Corbett about getting Robbie to come to us. I am sure that Peter, who was watching the game, was pleased that he had agreed to let Robbie join us. The start of the second half was much more equal as we gave as good as we got. After about 70 minutes we got a corner and Charlie Innes fired in a great ball that I connected with to put us 2-1 up. I took myself off not long after this as my legs were seizing up on the muddy surface. Buckie equalised with minutes to go and the game ended 2-2 which meant that Caley had won the league by a point. There was a donation dropped in to our dressing room by a relieved Caley official at full time and we did not hesitate in drinking the donation. We had played against the second-best team in the League and put up a great show against them and for us this was a good end to the season. This was encouraging for the start of the following season.

During the close season I got speaking to Alex Caldwell who was coaching at Elgin City under Steve Paterson. I knew Alex first of all when he was at Dundee and I was across the road at United but was formally introduced to him by one of my team mates from Wigan Bobby Hutchinson.

Bobby was at Dundee with Alex and Bobby asked Alex to be the Godfather to his son. I drove Bobby from Wigan to Aberdeen for the Christening ceremony and that was when I first met Alex. Alex had been a successful Manager at Lossiemouth but had joined Steve at Elgin. As Alex lived and worked in Inverness it was difficult for him to make it to training in Elgin and Steve was very helpful in making the move happen.

The two of them were to be re-united in later years as they steered Inverness Caledonian Thistle to that historic "CaleyThistleGoBallisticCelticAreAtrocious" Scottish Cup win.

I asked Alex to take on all the Coaching of the team and this left me to concentrate on the Commercial side of the club. I was still registered as a player but was having more problems with the knee I damaged in the car crash. I struggled to train 2 nights a week and also play on the Saturday. I went and seen my doctor and was referred to Raigmore and they X-rayed my knee. The results showed that the cartilage was damaged. It was decided that they would need to operate and remove it and a piece of bone that was also floating around the knee.

I was lying in my hospital bed after the operation with my leg all bandaged up and a Clach supporter who worked there, big Robert MacKenzie the darts player, popped his head in and said "What is up with the leg Jim, burns?" I asked him what he was on about and he told me that a fire had ravaged the main Clach stand and it was damaged beyond repair. There were a few rumours going around about the cause of the fire but I had the perfect alibi as I was laid up in hospital.

As we did not have dressing room facilities at the start of the season, we had to play all our games away from home to begin with. The area where the old stand was located was sold off to property developers who built houses with the club receiving money which went toward paying some of their debts.

After my knee operation I decided it was time to hang up my boots and take a back seat and concentrate on Managing the team. I would only list myself in the team if it was a real emergency.

When we had played Rangers, Walter had asked who the young lad in our midfield was as he looked a good prospect. He was asking about young Robbie Williamson, who was Rangers daft. Walter said he would like to have a look at the lad and would he be available to come down to Ibrox for a trial. I spoke to Robbie and asked him if he fancied going to Rangers for a week and he thought that I was taking the piss. I eventually persuaded him that I was serious and that Walter had asked me to ask him.

We got some dates arranged for the trial and Robbie arranged to get some time off his work. He did well when he was there and Rangers had some brilliant young midfield players there at that time. I was delighted for him when Rangers said that they would like to sign him on and would we come down for signing on talks.

We arranged to go down when Rangers were playing Celtic at Ibrox and our Group consisted of myself, Robbie, The Chairman Willie MacLennan and one of my work colleagues Norrie Hayden. Norrie was a massive Bluenose and we dressed him up in a Clach blazer and tie for the day and said that he was one of our Directors. Norrie passed away a few years ago but he always told me that was one of the best days of his life. I always asked, "Which part, being a Clach Director or sitting in the manager's office at Ibrox?"

The day started with us entering the front doors of Ibrox and being escorted up the stairs to the Managers Office. There we were greeted by Walter who took us in to meet Graeme Souness. Graeme was dressed in his training kit and shorts and was sitting with his feet up on the desk when we came in. What a cool customer he was and I mentioned to him that I had met him in Hong Kong when Liverpool had been out there. He recalled the trip but did not remember me. Probably because he had not come out with us all that night.

I asked him how he thought the game would go today and his reply was "We have better players than they have so if we play to our strengths we should win". He then left with Robbie and left myself, Willie and Norrie to sort out the transfer fee with Walter. The talks went something like this. Walter said "Okay Jim, what are you looking for?"

I said what we were looking for and he wrote that down, I then asked for a similar amount after he played 20 games and he wrote that down. I then asked for a similar amount if he played for Scotland which he wrote down. He said is that everything? I then said we would want 10% of any fee if he

Clachnacuddin F.C. 1987-88

Back Row L to R: Ivor Robertson, Brian Davidson, John MacDonald, Joe McIldowie, Steve Mitchell, Kenny MacKenzie & Ian Manning (trainer)

Middle Row L to R: James Oliver (manager), Alan Clark, Robbie Lowe, Gavin Dearie, Derek Rudkin, Charlie Innes, Gus Craib & Alec Caldwell (ast. manager)

Front Row L to R: James McVinish (coach), Martin Munro, Robbie Williamson, Keith MacLeod, Andy Gillan & Ron Murray

was transferred.

Walter then read back everything to us and said to me is that it, are you happy with that? I said yes, he looked at Willie and said are you happy with that and Willie said yes. He then turned to Norrie and said are you happy with that and all Norrie could get out was "Mmmmm" and a nod of the head.

With that completed we were taken to a restaurant within Ibrox where you could have had anything you wanted to eat. The waitress came over and asked us what we would like and Willie MacLennan asked if they did Scotch Pie and Beans. The waitress looked at him horrified and said I will see if we can get that for you sir and then he asked her if he could get a big ladle full of beans. By this time Robbie had rejoined us and he said, "Look over there, that's Davie Cooper."

The Chairman said "Who is Davie Cooper?"

Worse was to follow from the Chairman as we were sitting in the Private box.

There was the 4 of us and another 4 gentlemen obviously supporting the team in blue. With a couple of minutes of the game gone Celtic took a shock lead and Willie jumped up and cheered. No one else in the box cheered and Wille said Did I not tell you I was a Celtic supporter? I thought we were going to get thrown out but thankfully Rangers came back and won 4-1 which probably saved the day. All in all, a good day out at Ibrox and we came up the road having secured what we thought was a good deal and a great opportunity for Robbie.

The switch to full time football did not suit Robbie and he became homesick. This was something that I could sympathise with as it was hard for me as youngster away from home. I tried to speak to him and persuade him to stay and give it a chance. I had several calls with Rangers Reserve Team Manager Jimmy Nicholl at the time as we tried to find a way to make him feel more at ease. However, Robbie is a very determined person and he had made up his mind and he came back home. He came back to training at Clach but was being tapped by Ross County and as Clach were now unable to pay wages we could not hold on to him. One night at training he lashed out at one of the other players and I sent him in to the dressing room and I knew that he would leave after that. Robbie joined Ross County and had a fantastic career there. We made up our differences and he even asked me to be the Chairman of his Testimonial Committee when he was granted one by Ross County.

One of my other tasks at Clach at this time was to be the Editor and Producer of the Clachnacuddin FC Match Programme. I was still working at Nigg Oil Fabrication Yard and the photocopier at work was doing overtime. I enjoyed the whole process of pulling the programme together and I have kept several copies of the programmes in my collection of football memorabilia. I even kept the draft programme that I sketched out on my drawing board at Nigg.

After the club had taken in a considerable sum from the Rangers game and had sold off a big area of the ground the Committee kept saying to me that there was no money for players wages and that the club would have to stop paying them. This would mean that the players would become Amateurs and would be free to leave if they wanted to. In my first season there as a player we were paid £20 per week and got an extra £5 bonus if we won. I changed that to £5 wages and £20 bonus if we won and having 20 signed players it cost us £100 a week to keep them as semi-professionals. This went on for a couple of weeks with the committee saying that they could not afford it.

In my frustration, I had a go at them in the press. The Committee asked to see me and they offered me £100 a week to not go to the press about what was going on. I found this to be unbelievable as that was how much it cost to keep the players semi-pro.

I wrote a proposal to the Committee about what should be done to turn around the fortunes of the club. I still have a copy of the document and it was a 12 point plan of how to go about it. I think I lost the battle at point 1 as it read: "Point 1 – The present Committee to resign."

Maybe I should have kept that under my hat until I got them interested in what was proposed. The bottom line was that they did not agree with what I was proposing so I resigned as team manager. I was still signed as a player so I requested that I be released from my contract.

Being Captain, Player Coach, Player Manager and Manager of such an iconic club as Clachnacuddin FC was a real honour and it hurt me having to leave in such a manner. It was, however, not to be my last involvement with the Lilywhites.

A selection of Clachnacuddin programmes

The template and the first programme

Chapter 15

Balintore

After leaving Clach I felt like I could get back on to the park again as a player although not in the Highland League where the twice weekly training and game on a Saturday would be too much. I was approached by Balintore FC Manager Willie MacDonald whom I had played with at Invergordon back in the 76-77 North Caledonian League winning team.

In 1981, I played in the game to officially open the new football pitch at Balintore. The club had been given grants to build a brand-new pitch with dressing rooms on the hill above the village. The team that was invited to open the new pitch was the local Highland League team Ross County and I really fancied our chances as there were a lot of good players in our team. We beat a strong Ross County side 2-0 on the day, and I had the honour of scoring the first official goal at the new park. It was a free kick from around 25 yards which I got up and over the wall. In the second half we got a second from a William Ross header from a corner. On the Wednesday night we played a strong Elgin City side and beat them 2-1. I was just back from Wigan at the time and was free to play. I had played well in both games and both clubs had stated an interest in talking to me but I was destined for Montrose.

Willie and Allan Stainke, another member of that Invergordon team, were

Balintore F.C. line up before their match v Ross County to open their new football park in 1981

Back Row L to R: Sponsor, Ian MacDonald (manager), William Skinner, Robert Allan, William Ross, Willie MacDonald, James Oliver, William (Chats) Ross, Andy Barr, Stephen Paterson & Philip Macpherson (ast. manager)

Middle Row L to R: David Skinner, Alan Stainke, David Ross, Graham Skinner, John ?, Gordon Skinner

running the Balintore team in the North Caledonian league. This was my village team and they had not won the league yet in their current format but had come very close to it on several occasions.

Willie asked me if I would like a game for them as they were playing Ross County on Saturday at Dingwall and they were short of a few players. I felt OK and said I would be delighted to do so. When Willie named the team, I was down for playing right midfield and the thought of chasing a young Ross County midfielder back and fore was quite daunting.

When we got out on the pitch and the teams lined up, I looked to see who was playing left midfield for them and to my horror it was Donald Mackay from Brora. Donald was one of the most talented players to come from the Highlands. He had been a brilliant player with Brora and could have played at a higher level than Highland League if he had wanted to. He was a home loving guy and was happy to stay in the Highlands. Donald was a few years younger than me and I thought I was going to be in for a tortuous afternoon. After about 10 minutes the two of us were standing next to each other and Donald, being a red head, was not enjoying the sunny weather and he was looking like a burst tomato. It was great for me to realise that he was even less fit than I was and with the help of a very fit Gordon Skinner in front of me and a very fit Gordon Lowe behind me I managed to finish the game. It was great to be back playing and it is without a doubt the best part of football.

As I was still working in the Drawing Office at Nigg I was able to attend the training at Balintore after work one night per week and usually stayed over at my parents. Willie asked me if I would help with the training and I was delighted to help out. We had a young lad who was about 8 or 9 who would attend the training with his father and we encouraged him to join in on some of the exercises. It was clear that this young lad had great timing and he went on to have a great career in football. This was young Richard Hart who went on to play for Inverness Caley Thistle, Ross County and Dundee amongst other pro clubs. His father, also Richard, was a phenomenon as he played well in to his 40's. I recall telling someone that as a young kid I used to watch him playing and then 10 years after I retired, I was still watching him play.

At the start of the following season, we assembled a very good squad. As I was travelling up to the games most Saturday's it made sense to fill the car. There were a number of players in Inverness that were available and we added them to an already strong local squad. I continued to take the team for training and we were scoring lots of goals and playing great attacking football.

That season we only lost one game as we won the League for the first time in the club's history. We beat a strong Wick Academy 5-1 to capture the title and spark off a night of celebrations in the village. In the end we won the league by quite a few points. It was great to be part of the team that won the League for our village for the first time but at the end of the season I was to move again.

However, we still had to have our end of season trip. This year we were going to Benbecula to play the local team. The connection between our village and the island of Benbecula was that one of the villagers Mac Skinner had married a girl from the is-land and had moved there to live.

The bus picked us up in Inverness and we had a few beers on board as we made or way to Uig on the far end of Skye. Once there we had to board the Caledonian Mac-brayne ferry to take us across the infamous Minch. The water was flat calm as we stepped on board and immediately Gary "Nipper" Mackenzie felt seasick. We were still moored to the pier and he was being sick. After a fairly smooth sail across the Minch, we were met by a local bus which took us straight to where the game was to be played.

We got changed in a hotel beside the pitch and when we came out, we found the longest pitch I have ever played on. It was as if they had put a set of goals at either end of the island. I was playing at the back in this game and I recall a ball coming at me and I thought I would pretend to head it but let it run through to our goalie. Our goalie was Ian MacGregor who was around 6' 4" tall but when I looked round, he looked like a dot in the distance and suffice to say the forward got to the ball before him. I can't re-call the score that day, but I think we were well beat.

Following the game, we went straight to the pub and the session was on. As we had got changed at the Hotel beside the pitch all our overnight bags were taken to the houses where we were staying.

As we had no idea where these houses were, we were paired up with someone who knew which house we had to make our way back to. I can't recall much about the Cei-lidh that we attended but I do recall falling a couple of times at the side of the road on our way to it.

Balintore F.C. North Caledonian League champions 1989-90
Back Row L to R: Alan Stainke (ast. manager), Donnie Morrison, Robert Allan, Albert Allan, Ian MacGregor, James Oliver, Eoin Ross, Graham Skinner & Willie MacDonald (manager)
Front Row L to R: Gordon Lowe, Ray Tolmie, Gordon Skinner, Lennie Fraser, Charlie Innes & Gary MacKenzie

Next thing I remember was waking up in a dark room bursting for the toilet. I could not find a light but I could see the window and that had to do! I awoke a few hours later and there was light in the room and I seen that there was an en-suite in the room and then I started wondering where the hell was I. I put on some close and ventured out of the room and came in to a kitchen area where a woman was cooking over the frying pan. She was in a dressing gown and I was thinking where the hell was I. Next thing she said "Good Morning Jim how are you today?" I started to say "I'm not sure. Where am I?" when from the other side of the room I heard a few of the Balintore boys and the woman's husband roaring with laughter at my disorientation.

The guys had helped me home and had thrown me in to the bedroom while they car-ried on drinking. One of the guys said to me that they could not understand how I got so drunk as I can usually hold my beer but that night, I got drunk so easy. Graham Skinner our Captain said that he had looked after me as I kept falling down and he had to keep lifting me up. I said to him that it was his fault I was feeling so sore. If he had left me on the ground, I would not have been able to fall again.

I had spoken about Graham (Coochie) Skinner early in my football story as we had made our Carnival Cup Final debuts together as 14 and 15 year olds under John Jackson's coaching. Graham is without a doubt one of the best football players I have ever had the pleasure to play football with. There is no doubt in my mind that he could have been a top professional football player. Due to his family being faithful to the church he was unable to attend the Ross County training on Sunday mornings. He was a very skilful winger as a young lad but moved back to play the sweeper role and with his reading of the game he was immense in this position. The nearest that I can think of to compare him with is Dave Narey of Dundee United and Dave is the best player I have ever played with. I can't give Graham any higher compliment than that. However, I have told him not to pick me up when I fall again.

That was not the end of the shenanigans on our Benbecula trip as we then had to make the long journey back home from. As we loaded up the bus with a few supplies of beer we were in good form. When we were on the boat sailing back to the mainland Willie the Manager fell asleep and I took off both his shoes, took off one of his socks and put it back on top of the other sock then put his shoes back on.

When he eventually woke up and noticed that he was missing a sock he went crazy and was asking everyone where it was. He eventually blamed Nipper for taking off his sock and throwing it overboard and this theory was kept going by us all the way home. When he got home and was taking his sock off, he found the other one and burst out laughing. Someone let the cat out of the bag about who was to blame for this and he apologised to Nipper. What a great trip that was and we had one more adventure to do before my time with Balintore was up.

Some bright lad came up with the idea of dribbling a football up Ben Nevis for Charity. The charity chosen was the Hillsbrough Disaster Fund. On a Saturday morning we as-sembled at the foot of Scotlands highest mountain at around 10.00am. The only prob-lem for me was that I had been at a Stag Night the night before and had got around 2 hours sleep before being picked up by the bus in Inverness. The ensuing 8 hours or so were the most physically demanding times of my life.

I had prepared a haversack with plenty of food and more importantly fluids for the trip. With a few hundred feet to go myself and Ian "MacSpooch" MacDonald were cut adrift at the back of the group. One of the other lads had taken my well stocked rucksack with him to help me. MacSpooch and I stopped again to try and get a breath and we were close to saying "Bugger it" but between us we had been pledged over £1000 pound to complete the task.

It wasn't, however, the amount of money that would have been forfeited had we not completed the task that concerned us at that moment. It was the stick that we would get in the pub from the others for the rest of our lives that drove us on. Another thing that kept me going was the can of Tennents lager that I had put in the very bottom of my rucsack.

As we trudged up to the top of Ben Nevis we made or way to our group sitting there. I could not speak and went straight for my rucksack and dug deep to find my can of la-ger. My tongue was welded to the roof of my mouth at this time and I could practically taste the lager. I can still feel the overwhelming horror I felt as I realised the can was empty. It was one of the most horrible feelings I have ever felt. By this time the guys had realised that I was not going to be happy and were starting to disperse. If I had found out there and then who it was, I may have thrown them off the top of the moun-tain. It was a very quiet trip back down the mountain but I came round once I had my beer at base camp.

David Skinner, who was our Chairman at the time, wrote a piece about our Fund raiser up Ben Nevis and it was captured in the Seaboard Times for posterity. He also gave me a big clue as to who the culprit was that drank my beer. I shall have revenge one day!!

Great times making history for our village team and having some brilliant times along the way.

DRIBLE UP THE 'BEN'

Much has already been written about our recent sponsored dribble up Ben Nevis. Some of the stories were not strictly accurate so here is the facts from someone who was there !

The Object of the event : 1) To dribble a football all the way to the top of Britain's highest peak.

2) To raise money for Balintore F.C. and the Hillsborough Disaster Fund.

The 'Dribblers' : Gordon Lowe, Gordon Skinner, James Oliver and 'Nipper' Mackenzie.

The 'Sherpas' : J.F.Ross(sponsored), MacSpooch, David Skinner.

On a magnificent sunny morning at the foot of the 'Ben' in the presence of the 'P & J' photographer, our squad prepared for the task ahead. James Oliver fresh from a stag night three hours previous and Messrs MacSpooch, Skinner and Ross immaculately turned out having just left the North Caledonian League Dinner to catch the bus to Fort William. James Oliver (hereafter referred to as J.O.) borrowed his fathers cine camera, took a two minute presentation shot of the 'start', left the camera in the 'ON' position and so ended filming for the day ! I can also report that his early attempts to extract sponsor money from fellow mountaineers on route to the top were nothing short of embarrassing - his 16 stone frame being the only reason he did not get thrown off the mountain.

After about fifteen minutes the squad split into two groups. J.O. and MacSpooch went at a leisurely pace at the rear with the rest complete with packs some distance in front. It was then we discovered just how organised J.O. was (as we were carrying his pack for him). Sandwiches, crisps, lucozade, mars bars, beer and spirits (medicinal). Well there was no point in going to all that trouble, not to mention expense, for nothing - so we did the decent thing and ate/drank the lot (except the can of beer).

The road to the top was a long hard slog. We treated fellow mountaineers to a few well known football songs on the way, made friends with 'Cornflake' the dog who we seemed to pass a thousand times, and generally asked ourselves what idiot suggested that we did this in the first place.

Contrary to newspaper reports we did not have a game at the top of the mountain. Only Davy Skinner was fit to anyway.

As the first party reached the top bets were taken as to when/if the two tailenders would reach the top.

BETTING : MacSpooch (within the hour)   - 3 to 1
: J.O.   (same day)   - 500 to 1

The 'Bookie' won. When both were passed by some guy cycling to the top - their egos would not allow them pack in.

DRIBBLE UP THE BEN (Cont'd)

For the last 100 yards MacSpooch triumphantly marched to the
peak. J.O. was on all fours with only one thought in his head
- that can of beer !
Who mysteriously drank it we cannot say for fear of repercussion&
but we do know a well known joiner from Ross Crescent who could
help with enquiries. As this is a family programme we cannot
print J.O.s initial reaction.
The road down the mountain was somewhat uneventful in comparison
We all made it safely to a local 'resting place'. A fair amount
of money was raised and our special thanks go out to one
GORDON LOWE Esq., the *!*!**!! who thought of the idea in the
first place!

****

THE MANAGER says ....

We started training a few weeks ago in view of the hectic
schedule of pre-season friendlies. With the highly successful
trip to Benbecula and the more challenging match against
Falkirk last thursday evening now behind us we look forward
to entertaining Dunfermline tonight. To get teams of the calibre
of both Dunfermline & Falkirk to play at Balintore is a
tremendous boost not only for the players involved but the
community as a whole.
I can assure the supporters that the team that Alan and I will
field tonight will not let anyone down.
In the pool of players listed below you will notice one or
two unfamiliar names but players nevertheless I hope you will
give your wholehearted support in the months ahead. Big Iain
MacGregor, our goalkeeper, will be missed tonight but once
again we have secured the services of a more than capable
deputy - Graham Stewart.
POOL : Graham Stewart ; Gordon Lowe; Lenny Fraser;
Robert Allan; Graham Skinner; Gordon Skinner; Donnie Morrison;
Raymond Tolmie; Gary 'Nipper' Mackenzie; Charlie Innes;
James Oliver; Richard Hart; Rab Lockhart; Alan Brindle; Hugh
Taylor; Mark Stainke; Martin Faulkner.

****

On top of the world - well, Scotland at least.
The Balintore Ben Nevis Dribblers
Back: Jeff Ross, James Oliver, Ian Macdonald
Front: Gary MacKenzie, Gordon Lowe, Gordon Skinner

Chapter 16

Inverness Thistle 2nd Team

I was approached by Brian Black, who was Manager of Inverness Thistle FC, to see if I would be interested in running a reserve side for them in the North Caledonian League. Thistle had no place for squad players and players coming back from injury to get match fitness if they were not getting a game for the first team on Saturdays. This was causing problems for the club in recruiting youngsters as well as they wanted to be playing on Saturdays as well.

I asked Brian how Jock MacDonald felt about this as the last time I had spoken with Jock about football was when we were returning from Parkhead after our Scottish Cup game. At that time, I asked him if Brian or I could have a go at taking the training as it was a bit outdated. Jock's reaction at that time was to banish me and no effort was made to offer me a new contract. Brian said that Jock was OK with his suggestion and I took this as vindication that my original suggestion given on the bus was the correct way forward. I asked for a few days to think about it and said how many players do we currently have that are available for the squad. The reply was 4. Brian told me that they needed to know by that Thursday as that was when they had to confirm to the North Caledonian League if they were putting a team in or not. He also said that the only way they would put a team in was if I would run it.

I spoke to John "Cha Cha" Innes to see if he would help me. John was a player at Brora as a youngster and I had met him way back then when I signed as an S Form. We had not been in touch for many years but I knew of him from the Amateur Leagues in Inverness and knew that he knew a lot of players locally. If we were to pull a team together very quickly then John's contacts would be vital. John said that he would be happy to come and help me and I contacted Brian and said that we would like to have a chat with him. As part of the agreement, I asked if we could have a bonus structure put in place that would go towards an end of season night out. I drew up an agreement and Jock agreed to it and we said we would look after the Jags 2nd Team.

So, on the Thursday night Inverness Thistle FC entered a team in to the North Caledonian League. The following night I was at a function in town and I was given a lift home by then Clachnacuddin Director Charlie Forbes. Charlie said that the club had got a new Board of Directors and investors and would I be interested in being considered for the position of Manager of the 1st Team. I had to tell him that I had given my word to Inverness Thistle earlier that week and that the night before they had put a team in the North Caledonian League based upon my promise to them. I was honoured to be considered for the position at Clach but eventually they went for an experienced duo in Roshie Fraser and Peter Corbett. I was pleased with my decision to keep my word as these guys were the best guys for Clach at that time.

My plan at Thistle was to attract young talented players to the club but first we had to get a team on the park. A number of the Inverness players who were at Balintore with me said they would like to join me at Thistle and we signed up Rab Lockhart, Nipper and Charlie Innes. In addition, myself and Cha Cha were signed up as players so that we could get an 11 plus a couple of subs for our first game. John got in touch with several players he knew from the Amateur league and we had the basis of a squad. Rab Lockhart was in and out of the team at Balintore but had been on St Mirren's books as a youngster and he had that Central Belt grittiness about him. I made him our Captain and he thrived on the responsibility. Rab had come up to the Highlands to work at Nigg and was in the Drawing Office with me and that was how I got to know him. He is now living in Australia and has made a great life out there for himself.

After about 5 games I was invited to give a report to the Committee of how the 2nd Team were doing. I was invited in to the Boardroom on a Training night to discuss how we were doing. At that point we were still undefeated and had beaten Caley reserves at Kingsmills 1-0 that weekend. The Thistle Boardroom was quite a dark forbidding place to be in on a Board night Jock was at the head of the table smoking his customary cigar and several others had also been smoking. Jock asked me how we were getting on and I reported that we had played so many games and were sitting top of the league. He said that is good but the problem I have is that you are top scorer. I replied that as we only had the bare minimum that I had to play myself and if I was going to be on the pitch and be in a position to score, I would take that opportunity. Some of the others laughed but Jock gave them the stare and they clammed up again. I think he reluctantly said, "Well done", though.

A young lad who turned up at training, as his older brother was with us, was Richard Hastings and we let him join in. This was another young lad who was destined to become a star player. Richard played many times for Inverness Caledonian Thistle and became a Canadian International.

The team to beat in the league was still Balintore and after narrow defeats from them home and away we ended up Runners Up in the league. Not bad for a team that had only 4 players a week before the start of the season.

We had done a good job in providing a place where players not involved with the first team could get somewhere to play and we played with the same ethos as all Thistle teams in that we wanted to play attacking football all the time.

We were, however, to have success in the Chic Allan Cup Final and this also threw up a story which reached the National Press. We played Wick Academy in the final at Brora and after the game ended 2-2 we added two goals in extra time through Rab and Charlie to take the trophy. We had a few beers in Brora and stopped a couple of times on the way back to Inverness before arriving back in Inverness with the Cup. We went to Relax and the cup was on the bar as we celebrated. The next morning, I awoke with a bit of a hangover and phoned Cha Cha and asked if he had the cup and he said no. I then phoned Rab and asked him if he had it and he replied no. The last time any of us could remember seeing it was on the bar at Relax. I waited until the bar was open and went down to ask the owner if it had been left there and he said that nothing had been left. He did however say that some people had been acting suspiciously around it. After some digging, we found out that some Caley supporters had been in that area of the bar and we heard that they had taken it and threw it in to the River Ness. What a disrespectful thing to do to any cup however what these cretins did not realise was that the cup was in memory of Chic Allan one of Caley's finest ever players.

I was given the name of the person who was responsible and I made a visit to his house on the Sunday night. His father was a staunch Caley fan whom I knew and I told him what had happened. He called his son downstairs and at first he denied doing anything and then he said that he had heard it had been taken and thrown in the river. We got in my car and I asked him to show me where it had been thrown in. The River Ness was in full flow as it was in the winter time and there was no way of wandering

■ Lifting the cup has a new significance for Thistle reserve team boss Mr Jim Oliver and diver Mr Ian Brand.

Divers win back the cup for Thistle

□ BOB MACKINNON

DIVERS from the Alness firm of Sureclean Marine — after a bone-freezing, hour-long search of the River Ness bed — yesterday recovered the Chic Allan Cup.

The trophy, won by Inverness Thistle's reserve team last Saturday after they defeated Wick Academy in the final, was removed only hours later by a sneak thief, from the Relax Bar in Inverness, where the players were celebrating their victory, and cast into the nearby fast-flowing river.

Team boss Mr Jim Oliver, delighted with the recovery operation, said: "To get the cup back makes me feel even better than I did when we won it.

"If it had been washed out into the Moray Firth and lost forever, it would have been a tragedy."

The trophy was presented in memory of Chic Allan, one of Caley's all-time greats, who died in an accident during the 70s.

Mr Oliver said: "We are deeply grateful to Sureclean Marine, who gave us their time and equipment free of charge. The lads involved worked an extra three hours on their last shift to make the time available.

"Mike Rizza and the staff at Relax also provided us with considerable help which aided the recovery operation."

The diving team of operations manager Dave Sinclair, Ian Brand, Ian Davidson and Nick Hunter, are mainly employed at the Invergordon supply base on oilrig inspection work.

A police spokesman at Northern Constabulary HQ confirmed that a person had been charged in connection with the incident and a report would be going to the procurator fiscal.

The Sureclean divers help us to win back the Chic Allan Cup

in to have a look.

The following day I contacted a friend who had a diving company and asked if they could do anything for us. He said that they were unable to do anything on that day but that he would try and get a team together on the Tuesday. On the Tuesday they had a diver in to the water around where it had been thrown in and he did sweeps across the river until he was around 100m down from where it had been thrown in. He had a radio and I recall him saying "What is the name of the Cup?" and we replied The Chic Allan Cup and next thing hi hand came out of the water holding the Cup aloft. There were a few of the guys who had played had gathered to see this and it was like winning it all over again. A huge thank you was given to David Skinner (Balintore FC chairman) who was the owner of Sureclean and to Dave Sinclair (a former Tain St Duthus team mate) who was the Dive Team Leader. The story reached the National Press and a very relieved Thistle 2nd Team Manager was seen holding the cup at the side of the river. As we were approaching the end of the season the Thistle 1st Team were struggling a bit while the 2nd Team were getting good results. One Saturday the 1st team were at home to Deveronvale in a game they would normally win and the 2nd Team were playing Caley 2nd team at Telford Street. We won our game 4-0 and the 1st team could only draw 0-0. As we had had an earlier kick off, we were back in the Baron Taylor Street Social Club well before the 1st team people arrived and our session was well under way. There were about 10 of us around the table and we had a £10 kitty. The Thistle Committee arrived and Jock made his way over to our table. He pulled up a chair and went to sit down beside me and I said to him that he could only sit at the table if he put his money in the kitty. In his usual gruff manner, he said that he could buy and sell every one of us at the table. I said it doesn't matter you have to pay to get in. How much is it he said and I said £20 a head and he threw in £40. He then said he wanted a word with me and that he wanted me to be the new 1st Team Manager. I told him that Brian had asked me to come to the club and that out of loyalty to him I would not take it. He told me that Brian will be leaving.

When it was clear that Brian was leaving the club, I was again asked by Jock if I would like to take on the role of 1st Team Manager. I said to him why don't you offer it to Dave Milroy as I think he would be interested. He did not think Dave was ready to stop playing yet and it was then I asked him if he would consider Jim Leishman. Jim had been out of football for a while after leaving Dunfermline and I had met him when he had taken a Dunfermline team up to play Balintore in a pre-season friendly. I had

The management team at Inverness Thistle FC
James Oliver, Dave Milroy, Jim Leishman and John Innes

spoken to Jim a couple of nights previous to this and asked him would he be interested in speaking to Jock about the vacant Managers position. He said that if Jock gave him a call, he would certainly speak about it.

After a couple of weeks without a Manager the whole of the 1st Team squad and the 2nd Team Management team were invited down to Tomatin Distillery on a Sunday afternoon. When we got there, it was to unveil Jim Leishman as the new Inverness Thistle Manager and Dave Milroy was unveiled as his Assistant. The Appointment caused quite a stir in Scottish football and to begin with the Thistle results picked up in the league. A number of things happened personally to Jim and as the season came to a close the results fell away again.

I thought that I was getting a call up for the 1st Team away to Huntly as they had quite a few injuries and Jim asked me if I was up to being on the bench. I said I would be delighted and I would have loved to have once more pulled on the Jags 1st team strip. At the end of the day, I think a couple of guys said they would be ok and my return to the first team and the Highland League was not to be.

The 2nd Team's season was coming to an end and I presented Jock with the information on what was due to the 2nd Team for their success that season as per our agreement at the beginning of the season. Jock said that he would not pay it even though he had agreed it. I don't know why he did this but I wasn't about to argue with him over it. My word is my bond and I used my own money to reward the players as I had told them what they were getting for each game.

I told Jim Leishman what had happened and that I would be leaving at the end of the season because of it. Jim tried to get me to stay but the damage had been done and I said that I would not be coming back the following season.

Time to move on again.

Chapter 17

Clachnacuddin 2nd Team

When it was known that Cha Cha and I had resigned as the Inverness Thistle 2nd Team management team, we were approached by the management team at Clachnacuddin to see if we would run their team in the North Caledonian League.

Clach were pulling together a big squad of players under Roshie Fraser and Peter Corbett. Roshie and Peter were Highland League Legends as players and had been Managers of Thistle and Caley respectively. As well as being steeped in Highland football they were also great lads who loved a laugh. They were tasked with bringing the glory days back to the Merkinch club. They had also secured the services of Alec Caldwell as 1st Team Trainer and were shaping up to having a better structure at the club. We were delighted to join and our remit was to bring on the younger players and also look after some of the first team squad who were needing games or were coming back from injury.

A number of the lads who had been with us at Thistle came with us as Thistle pulled out of the North Caledonian league as they did not have anyone to run the team. Early in the season we played Caley and beat them but a youngster in their team showed great promise. He had a great engine and a terrific left foot. We were told after the game that he was unsettled at Caley and that he would like to join us at Clachnacuddin. We spoke to Caley and we had to pay the princely sum of £50 to sign Stuart Golabek. Stuart went in to the first team group right away but he was not settling properly and we were told to ask if we could get the £50 back from Caley. We took him in to the 2nd team and spent a bit of time with him and he gradually came through to be a great signing and Clach eventually sold him to Ross County for a 5-figure sum. Stuart saw great service with County and Inverness Caledonian Thistle in subsequent years.

One of the benefits of joining Clach at this time was that there was some money in the club to pay for training facilities throughout the season and we were able to use the All-Weather Park at the Bught. The 1st team would train on one half of the park and we would train on the other half. We loved giving the players something to do with the ball as I believed that people will work hard without realising it if they are concentrating on an end product with the ball.

We had shooting practice, 2 touch and 1 touch games which sharpened up the players. We had a great group of lads and we really gelled together on and off the park. After each game we would have a sing song in the dressing room and we all sang The Righteous Brothers' "You've Lost that Loving Feeling" at full pelt.

Our season had started very well and we had played around 10 games and were undefeated. As there were so many players my appearances were now diminishing but I liked to have myself on the bench in case of emergencies as the average age was quite young. The North Caledonian League was a man's league and sometimes you needed an old head on the pitch to look after the youngsters.

We had played around 10 games and were undefeated when Calum Grant one of the clubs Directors, who is sadly no longer with us, invited former Watford and current England International Manager Graham Taylor north for a holiday.

Calum had worked with Graham at Lincoln City when they were younger. On the Thursday night Graham took both the 1st team and the 2nd team for a training session at the Bught all weather park. The following day he was a guest speaker at a fundraising lunch for the club. The other guest speaker was Scotland's International Team Assistant Coach Craig Brown. Quite a coup for the Lilywhite's to secure such prestigious speakers.

On the Saturday we were away to bottom of the league Dornoch in the league. I don't think I have ever seen a game like it in my entire football career. They had an experienced Goalkeeper George Clubb in goals that day and he must have had at least a dozen world class saves. In the first half as well as George having several unbelievable saves, we hit the woodwork at least half a dozen times. They had one chance at goal and scored. Half Time Dornoch 1 Clachnacuddin 0.

I got the guys in at half time and told them that all they needed to do was keep up the same performance and the goals would come. 2 minutes in to the second half and we had equalised and we thought that more goals would come. George Clubb had other ideas and continued to pull off save after save and we hit the woodwork a few more times. Then with about 5 minutes to go Dornoch got their second shot at goal and scored again to make it 2-1 to them. A few more chances and a few more saves and that was it 2-1 to Dornoch.

There was nothing I could say to our guys as they had played really well and there were no big mistakes at the goals we lost. We had come up against an inspired goalkeeper on the day and also had some bad luck in front of goal. I congratulated Jim McCue the Dornoch Manager on their win and went in to a quiet dressing room.

OK I said to them. well done on our undefeated record up till now, better to lose to Dornoch than to lose to one of our competitors. So, we are going

Clachnacuddin F.C. (1990) Ltd. was formed in May of that year after a group of businessmen, David and Alastair Dowling, Inverness Glass; Charles Forbes, local chemist; Colin Morgan, Jacobite Cruises; Calum Grant of Macraes Travel, Nairn; James Macdonald of Highland Industrial Supplies and solicitor Ken MacLeod bought the football and social club located in the Merkinch area of Inverness from the liquidator. Roshie Fraser was appointed manager and Billy Dingwall his assistant. They inherited one signed player and with only three weeks to assemble a team, managed to accumulate 26 points and reach the semi-final of the North of Scotland Cup, losing in a replay. Peter Corbett was appointed commercial manager and assistant football manager to Mr Fraser along with Alex Caldwell, who succeeded Mr Dingwall after he was forced to retire due to work commitments. A reserve side was established by Jim Oliver, John Innes and Andy Gillon, and already their groundwork with younger players is benefiting the club. Together with the junior weekly sessions under the guidance of all the club's coaches the club is building for the future. Much reconstruction work has also had to be done. Prior to 1991/1992 season, a new entrance, turnstiles, club shop and office, toilets and disabled facilities had to be built. The playing surface also required substantial work, and a boundary wall round the pitch was erected. A new roof was also required for the social club, which is run by steward Bob Murdoch.

Today's lunch marks the launching of a fundraising scheme to help finance the club's ambitious plan to create an all-seated, all-covered stadium.

SKOL

Ness Print Ltd., Inverness

CLACHNACUDDIN F.C. (1990) LTD.

PERSONALITY LUNCH
in aid of the club's grandstand fund

Guest speakers:

MR GRAHAM TAYLOR
England International Manager

MR CRAIG BROWN
Scotland International Team Assistant Coach

CALEDONIAN HOTEL, INVERNESS

FRIDAY, 31st JANUARY, 1992

The Fundraiser programme signed by guest speakers Graham Taylor and Craig Brown

Menu

Smoked Salmon
Donated by Strathaird Salmon
———o0o———
Home-made Scotch Broth
———o0o———
Roast Beef with Yorkshire Pudding
———o0o———
Selection of Fresh Vegetables and Potatoes
———o0o———
Fresh Fruit Meringue with Cream
———o0o———
Coffee

Complimentary Wine, Beer and Soft Drinks
Courtesy of Skol Lager

Liqueur Miniatures
Donated by Chivas Regal

Shortbread
Donated by Walkers of Aberlour

SKOL

Order of Play

Top Table introduction by
MC DAVID LOVE
———o0o———
Welcome to guests
PROVOST ALLAN SELLAR
———o0o———
MR DAVID DOWLING
Chairman, Clachnacuddin F.C. (1990) Ltd.
———o0o———
LUNCH
———o0o———
MR CRAIG BROWN
———o0o———
MR GRAHAM TAYLOR
———o0o———
Vote of thanks
MR DUNCAN MACPHERSON
Convenor, Highland Regional Council

SKOL

to celebrate our undefeated run up until now and get our song going and I want us to belt it out and drown out the cheering from the other dressing room. When we get up to the Eagle we will still be bouncing and be sure to say well done to all the Dornoch players.

The singing started and what a racket we were making and we kept it going. The Dornoch players were wondering what was going on as it should have been them singing. That game and one other cup game against Balintore were to be our only defeats of the season and I am convinced what we did after the game solidified us as a unit.

I was invited round to Calum Grants' house on Sunday by Calum, whom I had got to know well, to meet Graham Taylor. When I came in and seen Graham, I said to him "Don't you ever train my team again, we were undefeated until you took them for a training session". I then told them about the game, which Calum enjoyed as he was a native of Dornoch. Graham was an absolute gentleman and it was a pleasure to talk football with the two of them for a couple of hours.

One of the eagerly awaited trips of the season was the away match at Wick Academy. The Wickers were always great hosts and we never needed much persuasion to stay and have a few drams with them. At this time, we had a young lady driving the second team coach and the club that we went in to in Wick had a policy that women were not allowed in the bar. You wouldn't get away with that now. I tried to plead the case for her to sit in the corner as she would not be drinking anyway but they told me that if any women are in the bar, then they have to double the price of the drinks. She was immediately asked to go and sit on the bus. One of the players who had a bit of a fancy for her went and kept her company and they went off for a run in the bus. When they got back the bus would not start and we had to go back in to the club and wait for a replacement bus to be sent from Inverness. For years we used the excuse of the bus breaking down for being

Clachnacuddin F.C. 2nd Team - Season 1992-93
Back Row L to R: Steve Mackay, John MacLeod, Derek Arris, Andy Gilchrist &
George Stewart
Middle Row L to R: Andy Gillon (trainer), John Innes (ast. manager), Rob Lockhart,
Gary MacKenzie, Colin MacLeod, Steve ?, David Dowling (chairman) & James Oliver
(manager)
Front Row L to R: George Gaff, Mark MacKay, Gavin Dearie, ?, Karl Engel & Ralph
McIlveen

back late from Wick and this time it actually happened.

We continued to have success and eventually we reached a Cup Final. This was the first Cup Final under the new regime at Clachnacuddin and even though it was the 2nd Team it was very well attended by the Clach fans as the 1st team were away from home that day. We managed to win the Football Times cup at Alness against Invergordon and we brought the cup back to the Clach Social Club that night and had a great night. We would also win the PCT Cup in Dingwall against Golspie and were knocked out of the Chic Allan Cup by Balintore.

Our nearest competitors in the league were Invergordon and going in to the last game of the season we were one point ahead of them and we had to play them at home on a Tuesday night. Winning the league on a Tuesday night was a bit of an anti-climax but we did the business and that gave us 3 out of the 4 trophies available that season.

We had a terrific group of lads and a lot of them went on to have great Highland League careers and a few of them Mark Holmes, Stuart Golabek and Mark McCulloch went on to have careers in the Professional game. It was satisfying to have been involved in their initial development and see them going on to do well. I would like to think that I got my teams to play football the way it should be played with a bit of flair, a lot of determination and always with a smile on the face.

Something else had happened that season as my wife Pam became pregnant with our first child and because of that and increasing work commitments I decided that now was the time to take time away from the game. It was good to finish my playing/management side of the game on a high note with a league win and I had contributed with a number of vital goals when making emergency appearances. The highlight being an 11-minute hat trick against Tain after coming on as a sub.

This was to be my last playing role for a team of at least North Caledonian League standard but it would not be my last involvement with Clachnacuddin FC or indeed football.

Chapter 18

The Final Whistle

It was season 1991-92 that I decided to finish with playing for and managing teams in the North Caledonian League. I did however play for some teams in the Amateur Leagues in Inverness. Getting together with other former players to have a kick about and some fresh air before having a few beers was good fun. Once the beer flows and the dressing room banter begins it is a place where you need your wits and a sense of humour by your side. There are number of stories that I missed out from when they should have been inserted but I feel I can bring them up here as I start to anticipate the final whistle.

I have played for both Inverness Thistle and Inverness Clachnacuddin however not many people know that I was once stripped and ready to play for Inverness Caledonian in a Highland League Cup game at Telford Street. Caley were playing Ross County in midweek and I decided to go and watch the game. As I paid to get into Telford Street I was approached by Sandy Anderson who was part of Peter Corbett's back room team. He said "Jim do you have your boots" I told him to get lost as I thought he was joking. He then said that he was serious as the car taking their Aberdeen players through had been held up by an accident on the A96.

I did have my football boots in my car which was parked not too far away.

I went and got them and proceeded to the Caley Home Dressing Room. I walked in and a few of the boys looked at me with the bag and Billy Urquhart said I know we are short but I didn't realise we were that short. Cheers Billy.

I was named as a Trialist as I had regained my Amateur status and was not signed by anyone and therefore eligible to play. It was fun going out to warm up and hearing the Howden Enders reactions. As it happened the game was a 1-1 draw, and I did not get on which was disappointing as I reckon I would have scored. They put a young lad on with about 10 minutes to go and he missed two glorious chances which I am quite confident I would have buried. It would have been a great ending to this particular story. A couple of weeks later Peter seen me in town and gave me an envelope with my draw bonus money. I never did get my money back for paying to get in to the game.

An interesting story came out when I was speaking to Calum Grant a few years back. I was telling him that Alex Ferguson had come and spoke to me when I had my leg in plaster and said that Aberdeen had been watching me.

He said to me "Do you know how he never went for you?"

I asked him if he knew, and he said that he had heard from a reliable source that Jim McLean had put him off me. McLean had told Fergie that I was a load of trouble and that I was into guns! This was a reference to my shotgun experience while at Tannadice which was all above board and legal.

I sometimes wonder what might have happened if I was to work under Fergie. I reckon that he would have been able to get the best out of me. Anyway, it is all water under the bridge now and I am a great believer in what will be will be.

Another story of my time at Clach under Roshie and Peter was when we had our end of season trip to Glasgow. We took in a cup final, I think it was Aberdeen v Celtic, and Roshie and I got back to the hotel and the downstairs bar was closed. We could hear a noise from the 1st Floor and asked the Barman what was going on. It is a wedding function he said. Roshie and I made our way up to the 1st Floor and we identified the Groom and I said to him do you mind if we sit in the corner and have a few drinks as the bar down stair is closed. We told him we were staying in the hotel and that we were down from Inverness and that we would just sit there and sip away. He said that it would be OK so we did this but 10 minutes later we were at the head of the Conga and we were up dancing with Brides, Bridesmaids, Mother of the Bride and basically making ourselves part of the wedding group. I am sure that we are probably in their wedding album. Anyway, the next morning we were at breakfast and Roshie is still half pissed when this couple come up to him and say Hi Roshie How are you this morning? He said Who are you? They replied We are the Bride and Groom you were at our wedding dance last night.

I was working at Orion around 2009/10 when Orion came in as the main sponsor of the club and I was asked if I would help on the Commercial side of things. I did this and we helped pull the club back from the edge of extinction at the last hour. That started a few years of being involved off the park. However, being there gave me the chance to finish my playing career on a high.

It was around 2013 I was to play my last 11 a-side game and that was to be in the Clach Legends v The Wine Shed fund raising game that year. At the tender age of 55 I took to the hallowed ground of The Ferry San Siro to do battle with the Clach Supporters. The match was to raise money for the new Clean Sweep Stand at Grant Street. Several of the Clach Legends who had won the Highland League title in 2004/05 were in our team and a few of them were still in good condition.

Robbie Williamson who managed the 2004/05 team kept myself and Peter

Corbett on the bench so that we could go on and inject some pace and be impact players. The time came and the two of us went on and Ian Polworth and Bruce McGraw were withdrawn. Within minutes Peter scampered down the line and crossed the ball. It cleared the first defender and I cushioned it on my chest, let it run down over my belly and then rifled it on the half volley in to the roof of the net. That was it for me!! Scoring at the Ferry San Siro in a 10-2 demolition of the Supporters couldn't get any better. A great way to round off my football times on the park.

Nearly 50 years before that I had asked some lads if I could get a game with them. Little was I to know that my football journey would have me meet so many great people, many who have become life time friends, give me so many highs and lows and everything else in between. It felt emotional coming off that pitch as I knew I would never again play an 11-a-side game.

LILY LEGENDS	CLEAN SWEEP ALL STARS
Derek Arris	Evan Macdonald
Barry McGraw	Ross Miller
Herchie	Chris Stewart (coco)
Bruce McGraw	Sean Ross
Peter Corbett	Tubby
Neil Macuish	Sybol
John Seaton	Jock Leslie
Duncan Shearer	Dougal Leslie
Sandy MacLeod	Paul Glass
Steve (bisc) Macdonald	Ally Duncan
Stuart Golabeck	Paul Frewin
John (beano) Bain	George Fisher
Mike Sanderson	Martin Leslie
Martin (sinders) Sanderson	Rhys Mackinnon
Colin Mitchell	Paul Scobbie
Alex (chizzy) Chisholm	Mark Simpson
Andrew Lewis	Alan MacKenzie
Davie Brennan	Brian Duncan
John Bain	Gavin Mackie
Jim (jo) Oliver	Ryan Graham (questions)
Iain (polly) Polworth	
David (daisy) Ross	
Robbie Williamson—Manager	**Colin Mackenzie (shakey) - Manager**
Referee—Gavin Dearie	
Mascot—Arran McGraw	

What better way to end than with a goal against the Wine Shed?

Reflecting back on the opportunities I had I am sure I could have done better. There were a lot of times when my discipline let me down but there were also times when injuries at the wrong time did not help. There are a lot of players who were better than me who did not get the opportunity to play professionally so I am thankful that I did. I got to play professionally in 3 different countries and have met many brilliant people.

If I had tried harder to behave, I am sure I could have had a good career at a reasonable level. Are there decisions I regret? I would have to say Yes - but I don't lose any sleep over them. I am a great believer that our fate is mapped out for us and my route has taken me to where I am at present.

As I finish off this look back at my time playing football it is mid-April 2021 and we are just over a year in to the Covid-19 Pandemic which has

Slamming it past Evan MacDonald under the watchful gaze of the brilliant Alan Hercher

Having Herchie be the first to congratulate me on my last ever goal remains special. RIP Alan

paralysed the whole world.

I have just completed a year on Furlough from my role as Commercial Manager at Inverness Caledonian Thistle FC and a year ago I had not even heard of the word Furlough. I am thankful to the club for keeping me on Furlough for this period of time as it has allowed me the time to put down in words my football playing journey.

There are far too many stories to tell, many that would have me and others in a lot of trouble but it has been fun and given half a chance I would do it all again.

To everyone I have met on my football journey thank you for helping me make the memories that have been made.

To my wife Pam and my children Lauren and Gregor, thank you for putting up with a football fanatic.

JO